The CIA at Work

BY THE SAME AUTHOR

Viet-Nam
Benedict Arnold : Hero and Traitor
Bolivar the Liberator
Captain John Smith and the Jamestown Story
Gentleman Johnny
Saladin : A Man for All Ages
The Assassins
The Terrorists
The Invisible World of Espionage
Double Jeopardy

The CIA at Work

by

LAURAN PAINE

ROBERT HALE · LONDON

First published in Great Britain 1977
Reprinted 1978

ISBN 0 7091 6413 0

Robert Hale Limited,
Clerkenwell House,
Clerkenwell Green,
London EC1R 0HT

Printed in Great Britain by
Lowe & Brydone Printers Limited, Thetford, Norfolk.
Bound by James Burn Limited, Esher, Surrey.

Contents

Illustrations

PICTURE CREDITS

Popperfoto: 2, Associated Press; 8 and 9, the remainder American official.

1

From OSS to CIA

America's wartime Office of Strategic Services—the OSS—which was formed in October of 1941, was a vast and powerful activist Intelligence organization which was an outgrowth of an earlier, much smaller agency known as the Office of Co-ordination of Information.

As a functional Intelligence organization the OSS established the primary guidelines its peacetime successor, the Central Intelligence Agency, was to follow.

Prior to the establishment of either the Office of Strategic Services or the Central Intelligence Agency, the Federal Bureau of Investigation, a division of the United States Department of Justice, supervised internal, or national, security for the United States in cases involving violations of federal laws.

The FBI was, and had been since its founding in 1908, a federal, civilian, police organization but by the year 1941, with most of the world involved in a spreading worldwide armed conflict, the FBI's position as a national protective agency was not compatible with either the US government's increasingly complex overseas commitments or with envisaged demands shortly to be made upon the US government as a result of its foreign policies.

Nevertheless, because the FBI was empowered by law to act in cases involving claims against the United States, such as crimes on the high seas, conspiracies and espionage, and also as a result of an expanding demand for its services, it was allowed to send agents to foreign lands with the result that prior to World War II the FBI had begun to assume the appearance of an Intelligence as well as an investigative, national, US agency. But it was still, and always remained, a civilian law-enforcement facility, for which reason, among others, as war came closer to the western hemisphere, it was not suited to the requirements of a nation being drawn steadily closer to involvement in global conflict.

Subsequently, with the United States actively participating in World War II as an Allied combatant there occurred some overlapping of procedures between the FBI and the wartime Intelligence networks belonging to the armed services, but the FBI's civilian status to a great extent eliminated it from an active role in the field of international Intelligence during the war except within the confines of the western hemisphere, and as the military Intelligence organizations increased the scope of their operations, even Latin America, which at one time had been an FBI preserve, passed into the domain of the other Intelligence agencies, with the FBI becoming, once again, almost exclusively concerned with violations of federal laws within the national boundaries.

Otherwise, when war was declared on the Axis powers in December of 1941 and throughout the conflict which ensued, US Intelligence functions were carried out through armed-service networks. But again, there was considerable duplication of effort, as well as overlapping of procedures and authority, because each armed service, navy, army, air force, had its own Intelligence organization.

In addition, the US Department of State, and even the Treasury Bureau, had Intelligence units. Only two other war-time powers had such extensive Intelligence networks, National Socialist Germany and the Soviet Union. Of the three, Germany, Russia, and the United States, the nation with the least sophisticated and experienced Intelligence community, and the only one which had never maintained an adequate peacetime or wartime Intelligence service, was the United States.

The Office of Strategic Services was originally conceived as a civilian agency. William J. Donovan, its initial mentor, and US Word War II President, Franklin D. Roosevelt, envisaged the OSS as a variety of Intelligence-gathering, world-wide US government agency under jurisdiction of the War Department, modelled after the prestigious FBI, which would have perhaps been satisfactory except that in time of war, civilians, even the highly mobile and skilled ones which would serve the OSS, would be totally conspicuous, and handicapped, in a world of uniforms.

President Roosevelt and General Donovan persevered in their

effort to maintain the civilian status of the Office of Strategic Services, but regardless, a gradual and inevitable process of militarization took over.

Wars were not *fought* by civilians; they might be supported by them, but only people in uniform fought them, and, whatever else was envisaged for the OSS in its earliest days, it was not organized to become another non-combatant police establishment. It was created to abet conflict; clandestine, covert, secret war, but still war.

There were members of the Office of Strategic Services who deplored the militarization, but when the United States declared war on the Axis powers and General Donovan appeared in uniform, tacit acceptance within the organization was unanimous.

William Donovan was not new to the uniform. He had served notably in World War I. He was in fact one of only three Americans to hold the three highest decorations bestowed by the United States on its servicemen : the Distinguished Service Medal, the Distinguished Service Cross, and the Congressional Medal of Honour.

Not until the war ended in 1945, and the OSS was facing the same process of dismantling that so many other war-oriented adjuncts of government faced, did it revert to civilian status. By then there was no longer a need for uniforms, and also by then, in the view of many Americans, neither was there a need for a 'cloak and dagger' clandestine organization such as the OSS, which, at its peak wartime strength probably employed no less than 30,000 people, world wide.

As a matter of fact, citizens of the United States, lacking a tradition in espionage and having recently emerged from the most costly war in history, during which they had learned to equate Intelligence-gathering with Germany's *Abwehr* and *Gestapo,* were unsympathetic towards any variety of secret service.

Nor did it help matters that many US leaders and people of influence echoed the sentiments of Henry L. Stimson, US Secretary of State in the pre-war Hoover cabinet, who said in 1929, 'Gentlemen do not read each other's mail.' The United States had never before possessed a genuine Intelligence service. Most of its leaders, in uniform and out, with a few notable exceptions such as George Washington, took the Stimson view. In World

War I the US maintained an Intelligence system of sorts, which accumulated information largely by relying on British Intelligence services.

During the US Civil War the federal government had to a great extent relied upon a hired private detective agency—Pinkerton's—to conduct the Intelligence function. There had been no precedent for anything like the OSS, which was actually much more than simply an Intelligence-gathering facility; it was also a society of assassins, and an organization of propagandists, demolitionists, terrorists, underground organizers, infiltrators, forgers, anarchists, whatever it had to be to deter and damage the enemy. In its early days it relied heavily on the British whose centuries-long expertise in the Intelligence field was superior to anything found elsewhere. But the consensus which conceded the necessity for such an organization in World War II, did *not* concede any such need when the war ended. The US had never had to utilize such a peacetime agency, and most Americans, influential and otherwise, saw no need for it after V-E and V-J days in 1945.

Nevertheless, the traditional idea that Intelligence work was dishonourable, disreputable, and contemptible, was as *passé* in 1945 as the idea that the US, the leading world power after the war, could revert to its comfortable pre-war isolationist cocoon.

Also, the idea that an Intelligence service had one, and only one function, that of gathering and analysing information, had also been *passé* since the 1920s. Intelligence in the 1930s and 1940s had moved beyond the realm of simple espionage, and it would in all probability never again revert to that status.

The reasons for this change will become obvious in the ensuing chapters. Suffice at this point to suggest that World War II and its immediate aftermath introduced changes in every field vital to the progress, the lifestyles, and the security of every living human being, and as commerce, industry, society and science had to keep pace, so did the Intelligence function.

Nevertheless, national leaders in the United States shared with lesser individuals whose backgrounds in the US have traditionally been the same, an aversion to what they knew was a dirty, contemptible business; spying on people, prying into their personal and national affairs. Even the tragic and stunning lesson of Pearl Harbour did not make the correct impression, which was simply that if the US had possessed any kind of unified bureau for the analysis of Intelligence, the Japanese never could have successfully attacked, and destroyed as much of the US Pacific Fleet as they did on 7th December 1941.

The aversion, however, persisted. With the war won and the orthodox armed forces going through the customary reversions, the OSS, with no such precedent, did not revert; it had no basic organization to revert to. It was entirely war-born. As long as President Roosevelt lived (he died one month and four days before the German surrender in Europe in 1945), General Donovan's agency was secure against encroachment by the armed services, but the OSS did not enjoy the same relationship with Roosevelt's successor in the White House, President Harry Truman, whose view was basically that there was no longer any need for an Office of Strategic Services. He seemed also to concur with the armed-services chiefs that espionage should be a part of the military establishment, and that for all else the FBI would be adequate.

General Donovan, who probably knew more concerning espionage as practised by the Asians, Europeans, and Soviets than any other American, argued for the continued existence of the OSS against the beliefs of the US Joint Chiefs of Staff, Congressional committees, and others. He contended that a reversion to the prewar status for US Intelligence was unthinkable. He said time and again that what was needed was an independent agency, of civilian status, separate from army, navy, or air force control, to function in peacetime as an Intelligence organization whose responsibility should be the accumulation of Intelligence.

The reasons which lay at the root of the eventual dissolution of the Office of Strategic Services were many, but in essence they were all political. The United States at peace has rarely demonstrated the same degree of high resolve it has demonstrated in war. When General Donovan finally resigned to return to the practice of law in New York, the OSS was taken over by the War Department. Its demise was subsequently quite rapid. The name was changed from Office of Strategic Services to Strategic Services Unit, War Department. Later, it was changed again: Central Intelligence Group, War Department. Finally, the OSS was dead, and what superseded it was nothing more than another subservient agency of the War Department, and within six months the same inefficiency, conflict, and monolithic confusion which

General Donovan had predicted if the separate service arms were allowed to handle the Intelligence function, had so irritated President Truman, across whose White House desk flowed an inundating tide of disparate Intelligence reports, that he sent the same letter to his Secretary of State, James Byrnes, his Secretary of War, Robert P. Patterson, and his Secretary of the Navy, James V. Forrestal. In this letter he instructed these men, and one other, his military advisor, Admiral William D. Leahy, to form themselves into a National Intelligence Authority unit, so that '. . . somebody, some outfit . . . can make sense out of all this stuff'.

The function of the National Intelligence Authority, in less forthright language, was to plan, develop, and co-ordinate all Intelligence activities. Funding was to come from the regular services, and to assist the National Intelligence Authority there was the Central Intelligence Group. President Truman took the first step in creating the new Intelligence organization when he appointed Rear Admiral Sidney W. Souers as Director of Central Intelligence. Nevertheless, independence did not imply autonomy. Admiral Souers remained subordinate to the three secretaries of the navy, the army, and the State Department.

The purpose for which President Truman had created the National Intelligence Authority, so that Intelligence reaching him came through a central, collating agency, had been achieved, but Intelligence as knowledgeable people viewed it was considerably more than what was reported in foreign newspapers and through paid informers, most of whom had their own axes to grind. It required something superior to what existed in the Group, and through the Authority.

Before and during Admiral Souers's short tenure as Director of the Central Intelligence Group a number of critical changes occurred world-wide. From war the West had peregrinated to peace, then to 'cold war'. What had been an interlude of co-operation in wartime between the principal Allied powers in the West, and the Soviet Union, had become, by 1946–47, what it had always been in theory, an uncompromising ideological confrontation. The more distinctly obvious this became in the West, most notably in the United States, the more obvious it also became that in the face of this great and growing threat something much more sophisticated than a collating Intelligence agency was going to be required by the leading free nation of the world.

There remained many Americans, and President Truman was not entirely free of the taint, who still considered espionage in any guise as both distasteful and dishonest. There were also a number of Americans whose enlightenment had been expedited by what had occurred in Poland, the Balkans, East Germany and elsewhere. Their alarm overcame their distaste, and the result was a more liberal, or at least a more rational, view of Intelligence requirements.

There were a number of results of this change of attitude in the United States. One of them was that the Central Intelligence Group began to assume a degree of independence; army, navy, and State Department influence became less.

At the same time the agency's directors were changed. Admiral Souers was replaced in 1946 by General Hoyt S. Vandenberg of the Air Force, and in 1947 General Vandenberg was succeeded by Rear Admiral Roscoe H. Hillenkoetter.

During this same period the US Congress directed that the American defence establishment be re-organized, with the emphasis on improved efficiency through unification. Among the changes deriving from this action was the abolition of the Central Intelligence Group as a collating bureau, and the establishment of a completely civilian Central Intelligence Agency, which was to co-ordinate its efforts through the National Security Council.

The Council, which was designed to act as supervising affiliation, consisted of the President, the Vice President, the Director of the Office of Civil and Defense Mobilization, the Secretary of State, and the Secretary of Defence. The Council was established by the same act of Congress, in 1947, which also severed the last controls the military had over the re-organized Intelligence agency, by creating an independent *central* Intelligence facility, whose purpose was to collect and evaluate Intelligence, to keep the National Security Council informed of all US and foreign Intelligence activity, and to co-operate with the service-arms' undercover agencies.

However, the final break with the military was still not resolved. Admiral Hillenkoetter, first director of the Central Intelligence Agency, continued in office until late 1950, then was replaced by another military man, General Eisenhower's former Chief of Staff during World War II, General Walter Bedell Smith.

Not until February of 1953 did a civilian finally become

director. He was Allen Dulles, General Donovan's wartime Chief of Mission in Bern, a veteran Intelligence official with experience in both world wars, and the brother of John Foster Dulles, Secretary of State under President Dwight D. Eisenhower.

2

Defining the Indefinables

It was the National Security Act of 1947 which breathed life into an independent Central Intelligence Agency, making it an adjunct of the executive branch of the US government, with duties which were defined about as well as it was possible to define the functions of an organization whose purpose was to collect Intelligence, largely through indefinable and unorthodox methods.

The CIA was to advise the National Security Council. It was to evaluate information having any bearing upon national defence or national commitments, and it was to co-operate with other US Intelligence organizations.

It was *not* to participate in the formulation of policy. Allen Dulles, among others, particularly pressed for recognition and acceptance of this point.

Dulles's view of Intelligence was the traditional one: collect information, assess facts, specify the conclusions in a manner which would enable other people, or agencies of government, to act intelligently and—hopefully—wisely. But, he said, 'The Central Intelligence Agency should have nothing to do with policy.' Its function should be exclusively limited, he thought, to getting 'the hard facts on which others must determine policy'.

This was a traditional viewpoint. It was in great measure based upon the fact, and the premise, that opposition Intelligence communities adhered to a similar concept, which they did, with one exception, when Allen Dulles made his statement shortly after World War II. But as all else changed after that conflict, so also did the Intelligence role, and by 1961, the year of Dulles's resignation from the CIA, he as well as other knowledgeable Intelligence vocationists knew very well that between 1947 and 1961, few things had changed as drastically in theory and practice as the Intelligence function.

Perhaps the changes which obtained between 1947 and 1961 should have been expected, or at least anticipated. In every other field of human endeavour change had occurred. But less than a figurative handful of people had any idea what a Pandora's box technology would turn out to be in the areas of science, industry and commerce, let alone in the areas of Intelligence.

The same awesome technology which put men on the moon and which created spy-in-the-sky satellites, also fathered a veritable host of other astonishing devices.

The difficulty arose when the public, awed by photographs beamed earthward from Mars and Jupiter, were not informed that this identical technology had also sired an equally as incredible revolution in the realms of Intelligence.

The Intelligence community did not advertise. It never has. The result has been that people in general, those in positions of power, trust, and influence, and those on the streets, had no idea that the cloak-and-dagger image, the historic concept of espionage, was no longer totally adequate, nor entirely appropriate.

By 1961, when Allen Dulles resigned as chief executive of the Central Intelligence Agency, the writing was clearly on the wall. Ten years later, in 1971, it was even more evident. Every aspect of the human experience had drastically changed, including the demands put upon the accumulation and analysis of Intelligence.

Nevertheless, uneasy lawmakers in the US wanted to define the Intelligence function. They feared an autonomous Central Intelligence Agency in 1961 or 1971 exactly as they had feared it in 1947, when, in recognition of a need to define the indefinables, they had sought specifically to spell out how the Intelligence network was to operate.

They did not improve the 1947 specifications which, under the National Security Act of that year established CIA duties as those undertakings especially assigned under the law, and 'such additional services of common concern as the National Security Council . . .' should determine may be accomplished.

In Section 102 of the Act it was further stated that the CIA should be authorized 'to perform such other functions and duties relating to Intelligence affecting the national security as the National Security Council may from time to time direct'.

This was the key part of the Act—Section 102—responsible for so much that subsequently created the furores in the United

States and abroad. It was also, in the way it was worded, a tacit admission that there were definite indefinables. There had never been, and there still is not, any way to spell out a precise sequence of operations for espionage.

Section 102, then, placed full responsibility for CIA actions which might be considered as beyond the traditional Intelligence function, at the door of the National Security Council, but, since the gentleman residing at the White House is senior to all members of the Council, it was the President of the United States who had *carte blanche*. Nothing which subsequently aroused censure occurred independently of his decisions.

CIA involvements and undertakings were ordered by the National Security Council. They were sanctioned by the Secretary of State, the Director of the Office of Civil and Defence Mobilization, the Secretary of Defence, the Vice President of the United States, key members of the Congress, all of whom, in this area, were subservient to the President.

As the CIA grew, as its labours uncovered hard evidence of subversive infiltration in the United States and among the allies of the United States, additional committees were created periodically to investigate both the CIA, and the quite often spine-chilling, Intelligence it accumulated, but fundamentally, insofar as all power could be said to have been invested in one individual, that person was the US President. Also, when detractors of the Central Intelligence Agency denounced as illegal some aspects of the agency's involvements they either were ignorant of, or chose to affect ignorance of, Section 102, which clearly authorized 'such other functions and duties . . .' as the National Security Agency directed.

The National Security Act of 1947, then, although frequently challenged, remained, and still remains, the conceptual basis for the existence of a Central Intelligence Agency, as well as for the manner in which it has operated, and in 1977, as in 1947, while it is entirely possible to limit CIA power and activities, it still is not possible to define the sequences or the details of espionage, nor does it appear wise to do so, at least not until the lion has learned to lie down with the lamb.

As for control, and in fact despite what critics have said about the CIA, at no time has the agency ever been free of Congressional, executive, or other governmental scrutiny. In 1956 President

Dwight D. Eisenhower created a board of 'Consultants on Foreign Intelligence Activities', and subsequently President John F. Kennedy convened his 'President's Foreign Intelligence Advisory Board', to report on CIA efficiency and competence. 'Special Committees' have always been near at hand to examine, investigate, recommend, and advise, and as the agency's role as counterfoil to the Soviet Union's notorious KGB became increasingly active, public opposition to CIA growth and development proliferated even more rapidly than did the 'Special Committees'.

All CIA undertakings which were known or suspected were subjected to critical, and in most cases, derogatory, interest. US concern neither began nor ended in Washington; everyone, it appeared, had opinions. Many educators alleged that an Intelligence facility could become a threat to national, and individual, freedoms.

It was also said that since the CIA operated in a vacuum of silence, it had to be both menacing and sinister.

Generally, the consensus appeared to be as it had traditionally been among Americans: Intelligence was inconsistent with the ethics and principles of a free society. People were uneasy; many were downright fearful. There was certainly evidence that in other lands, notably Germany, Italy, the Soviet Union, the espionage apparatus had become a whole lot more than simply an Intelligence-gathering organization.

No one was required to be an authority to appreciate how successfully a great many tyrants had achieved supremacy, and had maintained themselves in power, through utilization of internal and external espionage.

It was unquestionably with this in mind that US legislators had prohibited the CIA to operate within the United States. '. . . That the Agency shall have no police, subpoena, law-enforcement powers, or internal security functions . . .' was part of the law which initially defined CIA status.

But none of this really removed the misgivings, and of course the secrecy which is necessarily a part of any Intelligence agency did nothing towards alleviating anxieties. Inevitably, too, the people who, for whatever reason, were adamantly opposed to the United States having an Intelligence organization, were clamorous out of all proportion to their numbers. But in general, it was the secrecy that made most Americans uneasy.

There was, and remains, the total silence surrounding CIA activities which Americans found most difficult to accept. The agency never publicized its triumphs, nor defended its failures. It has remained mute in the face of attack, and this policy has left it vulnerable to almost any derogation, a fact its ardent enemies, well-meaning and otherwise, have fully recognized and very thoroughly exploited. Revelations of any kind, even very belated ones which can seemingly no longer jeopardize agents or objectives, have never been publicized. At least not officially.

Nothing has demonstrated how effectively this policy of silence works against the CIA as the notorious Bay of Pigs Cuban invasion disaster of 1961. Anyone who cared to make the effort could ascertain without much difficulty that the Bay of Pigs episode *was not a CIA débâcle*, (clarification in a later chapter) but books, magazines, newspapers, in the US and worldwide, consistently put full blame for that infamous sell-out at the door of the Central Intelligence Agency, and never has the agency issued a denial.

The Soviet Union, European labour unions, Latin American political groups, university students anywhere, international terrorists, have consistently blamed the CIA for whatever required a scapegoat, without fear of denial. Everything, from meddling in the affairs of foreign nations—which it has done—to responsibility for poor skiing conditions at St Moritz, has been sources of vilification, the vilifiers knowing there will be no denial and no confirmation. Nor has there been.

In many areas silence in the face of an accusation has been equated with guilt. The most improbable charges have been levelled against the CIA, and the consistent policy of secrecy and silence has done harm. There does not appear to be any real alternative to the secrecy and silence which has accompanied CIA operations in most instances, nor does there appear to be a remedy for the uneasiness felt by people in a free society at having a large espionage organization in their midst. Among the nations of Europe people have over the centuries learned to live with a good many necessary evils, such as armies, navies, air forces, and espionage facilities, but notwithstanding, most free people would certainly prefer not to have to tolerate—and financially support—highly sophisticated and rather extensive Intelligence facilities. The difficulty appears to be that if people who *are* free value their freedom and their security, they must then include the tolerance of an Intelligence organization, and its support, in the cost of those cherished possessions. They must prudently and simultaneously hedge their Intelligence community around with every available check and balance, because, whether free people like the idea of having such an organization in their midst or not, they may be assured that the enemies of free people not only maintain such an organization for the exclusive purpose of providing the enemy with the information which will one day help him deprive free people of their independence, but the enemy has the largest, most costly, and in some ways, the most successful Intelligence establishment in history. The Soviet Intelligence apparatus numbers in excess of 250,000 people. Its satellite affiliates in Europe, Latin America, Asia and Africa number another 400,000. This is the adversary of the Central Intelligence Agency, whose comparative size, although an occasional source of loud lamentations among US politicians, most notably at election time, has never, even in the most halcyon days of General Donovan's wartime OSS, came anywhere near approximating the size of the Soviet Intelligence establishment.

Of course size has never been synonymous with either efficiency or success. Britain's wartime Special Operations Executive, an espionage-sabotage facility of very modest size, scored some very commendable achievements against its larger Axis adversaries, the *Abwehr* and the *Geheime Staatspolizei.* But that was a full generation ago; in those days it was still possible for nations of moderate size and strength to win wars and tip scales.

In 1950 the Central Intelligence Agency had a personnel roster of somewhat more than 4,000 people. During US involvement in the Korean War, the agency roughly tripled in size. These later employees, largely connected with the Clandestine Services division, were not, as one might assume, essentially occupied with the Korean War, although of course a strong element of them were. Generally, they were logistical people; geographic planners, political and social scientists, and the clerical personnel such an increase required.

By 1955, with Soviet aggressiveness embarked upon one of those cyclical epochs of obnoxiousness which seem to wax and wane as part of Soviet policy, America's Central Intelligence Agency began to assume the professional appearance it was to maintain for the ensuing two decades.

As its professional capability increased, as additional demands were made upon it by many sectors of the US government, and also by the free allies of the US, internal structuring commensurate with growth and requirements pushed the agency's size to the authorized manpower maximum of 16,500 people, among the several categories, with an approved budget of seven hundred and fifty million dollars.

For a nation which had seldom employed professional spies, and whose people were far from unanimous in their conviction that the free world needed such an organization, both the size and the cost of the CIA were shocking. As a matter of fact, as time passed, the agency's size was increased by statute, but even when there was a personnel composite among the several categories of close to 20,000 people—most of whom were administrative or technical—the CIA's total of authorized personnel was less than one tenth the size of the Soviet Union's KGB, which has been the CIA's—the entire Intelligence community of the free world—pronounced and unyielding adversary for thirty years.

There was, however, another aspect of CIA employment. For example, during the Korean War the United States effort to gather hard Intelligence in China, North Korea, and elsewhere within the neighbouring periphery, required the employment of a great many people whose racial and ethnic backgrounds made it possible for them to penetrate areas where no 'Westerner' could appear. Also, during the course of that war (1950–1953), the burgeoning clandestine services of the United States CIA functioned as had the corollary agency of General Donovan's OSS during the Second World War. In other words, the traditional function of an Intelligence establishment—the gathering, interpreting and analysing of information—was no longer the CIA's exclusive function; and as a result, in situations where neither orthodox US forces nor the armed elements of the United Nations membership could operate for any one of many reasons, the CIA had its hired spies, saboteurs, infiltrators, and in some instances, it also bought politicians, educators, North Korean defectors, and highly positioned professional people, all of whom aided the United Nations war effort.

It was these people by the hundreds, (by the thousands if one includes the highland tribesmen trained and paid by the CIA for missions of stealth and ambush) who raised the CIA's budget very considerably. But nevertheless, even when the cost of clandestine activity in Korea tripled the agency's budget, even quadrupled it, the clear fact remained that the successes achieved—as well as the failures—could not have been accomplished less expensively. Also, enemy Intelligence was costing more, and in many cases, producing less. The biggest blunder of the Korean War on the US side was the miscalculation of the Chinese attitude and, as in similar situations elsewhere, although the US leftist press successfully convinced most Americans that this error was a direct result of CIA inefficiency, as a matter of fact CIA hard Intelligence, gathered through its considerable Asiatic Intelligence network, had been keeping US Commander General Douglas MacArthur and others, including President Harry Truman, informed concerning a Communist Chinese troop accumulation along the Manchurian-Korean border for months before the Red Chinese struck. When General MacArthur, testifying before a US Senate Armed Services Committee in Washington, in 1951, stated that the CIA had said the Chinese would not intervene, he demonstrated a faulty memory. What the CIA had been reporting for a long time was that the Chinese were amassing an invasion force just over the border, that they certainly had the power to intervene, and were also much inclined to intervene. MacArthur's defence of his failure to heed the hard Intelligence was based on his reputation as an outstanding World War II commander in the Pacific, but even back in those days General MacArthur had refused to co-operate with any Intelligence organizations which were not entirely subservient to him.

The facts were clear : both the CIA and the US State Department had information as early as 1950 that the Red Chinese *would* intervene, if United Nations forces crossed the 38th parallel which divided North and South Korea.

Further, in army circles it was assumed there would be Chinese intervention if United Nations forces invaded North Korea. Also, on 3rd October 1950, more than a month before the Chinese poured across the border, 200,000 strong, to halt the United Nations advance, the United States government, and the CIA, received conclusive information through New Delhi, Stockholm and Moscow, that intervention would occur if United Nations troops crossed the 38th parallel. MacArthur was instructed to observe caution. Instead, he pressed the attack, and when Red Chinese troops were encountered, he threatened publicly to use his air power and his navy in an attack upon China. He was then removed from command, but the damage had been done.

Had MacArthur received CIA warnings? According to President Truman, General MacArthur was given a CIA report which stated that the Chinese *would* attack, seeking 'to immobilize United Nations forces, subject them to prolonged attrition, and maintain . . . the North Korea state in being'. At his appearances before the Senate Armed Services Committee, when General MacArthur was asked about the CIA in Korea, he made a very revealing statement. He knew nothing about the CIA because, as he said, 'The CIA doesn't operate under me.' And again : 'As far as I know . . . [the CIA] . . . was never in Korea.' The facts were, that the CIA's chief, General Walter Bedell Smith, went to Tokyo to confer with MacArthur concerning the lack of co-operation between MacArthur's Intelligence chief, Major-General C. A. Willoughby, and the CIA's agents in Korea. Of this matter MacArthur later said, '. . . I insisted . . . that the Central Intelligence Agency . . . would not act surreptitiously.' It would appear, then, that General MacArthur certainly *did* know the CIA was operating in Korea. But the gist of all this, clearly, was that the CIA did not fail in Korea. Its assessments and its reports *were* available to the Commanding General, and were either ignored by him, or were subjected to his ridicule, with very unfortunate results for the United Nations armed forces.

With the end of the Korean War, the CIA's value as a competent agency for the accumulation and analysis of Intelligence was established. However, the same people who were willing to acknowledge this fact were generally unwilling to accept CIA involvement in anything that resembled armed activity.

In the 1950s there were very few advocates of the premise that the United States should possess a clandestine organization which could face the Soviet Union's KGB in any area except that of gathering Intelligence.

It was abundantly evident throughout the '50s, that Soviet clandestine subversion had embarked upon one of its cyclical interludes, and that neither the armed force of small nations, its targets, nor the admonishing rhetoric of disapproving strong nations, were likely to prevail, without help.

The Soviet Union, in full recognition of the degree of change which had altered all facets of life and politics after World War II, correctly assumed that the United States was still thinking in terms of the Hitler war. The Soviet Union had, and the United States had not, realized that in the new epoch, the Intelligence function could be successfully utilized to achieve goals which armed invasion or intervention were unlikely to achieve as successfully. In a world weary of warfare, armies were anathematized and unpopular, but an Intelligence organization empowered to direct, fund, and actively support subversive uprisings, could succeed.

In Korea, in Indonesia, in Cuba, Colombia, Peru, and in Mexico where total victory was very narrowly averted, the Soviet Union's powerful KGB, which had become far more than simply an Intelligence-gathering organization since its inception, combined espionage with overt intervention on a massive scale, and in the United States belated counter-measures were undertaken, with the sanction of the National Security Council, resulting in the CIA being empowered to challenge the KGB. The moment this occurred, the CIA ceased being a traditional Intelligence-gathering organization. It also became the West's only strong defence against Soviet subversion.

The cost was immense, the successes were hard-won and not immediately clear, the failures were many, and the matter of creating secret armed forces in Communist-threatened nations, strained every CIA resource. But it was done.

The number of US officials at all but the highest levels who knew that the agency had embarked upon this new course was initially, very small, and it remained small during the time when the CIA was organizing its vast and very expensive world-wide Intelligence network, which included armed and funded secret armies, air forces, and navies.

The American voting—and taxpaying—general public knew practically nothing about any of this for a considerable length of time. Without much doubt if the information had become widely known, public reaction would have been predictably loud, long, and adverse. But there was another reason for secrecy. In the kind of clandestine war being waged by the opposition, revelations concerning CIA goals, techniques, and involvement could only have been damaging.

By the time the Communists were prepared to launch *coups* in such places as Asia, Latin America and the Middle East, CIA capability had proliferated to the extent that although the agency still maintained its manpower at the latest allowable limit (18,000) it also had satellite affiliates, and in many instances these organizations actually employed many more people than the parent organization.

These proprietory concerns were very expensive. There had to be a method for supporting them which would prevent the Communists from deducing their extent by knowing their cost. Also, again, public reaction was a factor in the secrecy which ensued, although, because the CIA's budget, established at 750 million dollars annually, was also underwritten by another source of revenue known as the 'Director's Special Contingency Fund', amounting to between 50 and 100 million dollars, in all probability the general public, watching for appeals for more money to the Congress, duly reported by the news media, would have been unable to detect a cause for outcry.

Defining costs, then as now, in order to make exact revelations, was impossible. Aside from the total silence surrounding secret operations in the '50s, and on into the 1960s, the matter of specific, or even general, funding, was competently obfuscated through expert and deliberate intent. In fact, the CIA's *actual* budget had been so highly restricted that when it was taken under discussion by the appropriate Congressional allocations committee, everything that was written down was subsequently sent to CIA headquarters at Langley, Virginia, and placed in vaults guarded by security police as well as sophisticated electronics equipment.

Nevertheless, from its relatively modest beginnings in 1947 to the present time the CIA has progressed from an Intelligence establishment costing less than most US federal agencies of a relative size to a very professional organization with worldwide tentacles, costing the US a minimum of one billion dollars annually, and, according to anonymous but knowledgeable people involved, actually costing closer to *seventy billion dollars.*

How is this done without an appeal for funds to Congress? Very simply; other government agencies such as the Department of Defence paid *their* budgets for additional millions of dollars, then transfer those funds to the CIA.

Congressional supervision of this money, which in total amount is larger in fact than the gross national product of most nations, has never been very successful. In the first place, very few people in a democracy have any idea how to put a price on espionage or subversion. In the second place, in accordance with the Central Intelligence Act of 1949, specific clauses concede the latitude which could become necessary, by granting to the agency's director the right to spend money 'without regard to the provisions of law and regulations relating to the expenditure of Government funds; and for objects of confidential, extraordinary, or emergency nature. . . .'

The question to be answered, then, was whether the United States in particular and the free world generally, profited adequately from this stunning outpouring of wealth? Was the first Queen Elizabeth's spymaster, Sir Francis Walsingham, correct or not, when he said, 'Knowledge is never too dear'? And what, exactly *is* the price of freedom?

3

No Defence Needed

Excluding the US Department of Defence—the 'Pentagon'—no other United States bureau of government has been so consistently vilified as the Central Intelligence Agency, within the US and beyond.

One is therefore entitled to wonder who serves this derogated Intelligence organization, and the answer is : more volunteers than it could possibly hire.

Its standards are high, and the demands made during periods of great stress are considerable. Not everyone is capable of fulfilling the requirements, or the demands. In fact, approximately eighty per cent of those who volunteer are not hired for reasons ranging from educational shortcomings to unacceptable personal backgrounds. Actually far fewer people than one might imagine have the requirements for espionage, or the qualifications to serve in the supporting categories.

The Clandestine Services, (under the Director of Operations) employ 6,000 people, 1,800 in secret subversion, 4,200 in actual espionage and counter-espionage. Otherwise, the agency has over 5,000 people in management, 1,200 in Intelligence analysis, 2,300 in processing information, 1,000 in technical assessment, 3,300 in support, etc., until the personnel ceiling is reached, and of the total, between sixteen and eighteen thousand people, 4,200 people are spies, with 1,800 involved in subversion.

In many instances the spies are not the most interesting people. Almost 20 per cent of the agency's professional employees have received higher education. At least 30 per cent of the Intelligence analysts hold doctorate degrees. Academic degrees are held by employees from 700 US universities and colleges, as well as 60 overseas universities. These degrees have been earned in 281 fields of specialization including political science, history, international relations, business administration, languages and economies.

Sixteen per cent of the agency's professional personnel have earned Master's degrees, 5 per cent hold PhDs, and 38 per cent of all employees are bilingual; 18 per cent can speak three languages, while 5 per cent can speak or understand six languages.

Members of the agency's research staff have contributed to the agency's 116,000-volume library. Scattered throughout the different bureaus are scholars of international renown, former diplomats, soldiers, famous scientists, as well as former foreign espionage agents and governmental officials whose careers would read like purest fiction.

Then, of course, there are the spies.

At one time the agency had in its employ a German national whose entire adult life had been spent in espionage. He was first recruited by the British 'in place', (meaning he was a national of the country in which he would spy), some years before the advent of Adolf Hitler.

He remained active and productive throughout the tumultuous years of Hitler's rise to power, and throughout the world conflict which followed.

After the war ended this man transferred from British Intelligence to the Central Intelligence Agency, and continued spying. He was never suspected nor uncovered. His career confirmed a rather disillusioning possibility: a spy, like a postal clerk, could conceivably retire to a cottage in the country after twenty or thirty years, with a modest pension.

Another aspect of espionage which this agent's career emphasized was that while a clandestine career may be colourful, that is only a minor part of the patience, shrewdness, caution, and the time-consuming dedication, coupled to complete anonymity, which is a part of every espionage activity. And to carry that a bit further, this particular secret agent, among the 4,200 espionage-counter-espionage agents serving the CIA, could accomplish very little without the co-operation of all those very talented and highly educated specialists at CIA headquarters, in Langley, Virginia.

A fair example of how this teamwork has produced results would be the Guatemalan affair, in the year 1954, when Jacobo Arbenz Guzman came to power supported by secret Soviet funds and technical experts. Arbenz did not achieve power by *coup*, which was unique in Latin America, and which was also unique among Communist-supervised political successes. In fact, Arbenz, like other Communist puppets, made a point of appearing to be a nationalist, until he was entrenched and his leftist supporters had assumed full control of Guatemala's military and police, then he pronounced himself a Communist. His was the first Communist government in the western hemisphere, something the United States could not have been expected to view with favour.

Even so, while the CIA at once began accumulating information, the United States Departments of Defence and State were slow to accept the suggestion that a Communist government in one Latin American country was an actual threat to other Latin American countries, especially since Guatemala was neither large, nor possessed of a modern war-making capability.

In neighbouring Honduras a Guatemalan named Carlos Castillo Armas, formerly a colonel in the Guatemalan army, and an avowed anti-Communist, was the spokesman for a group of Guatemalan exiles who, like himself, opposed Communism, and were especially opposed to it in their native land. Colonel Castillo needed arms for his small band of exiles. The governments of neutral Honduras and El Salvador, which also shared a length of border with Guatemala, did not consider the Castillo force as any real threat to Guatemala, or Arbenz, but Intelligence sources offered information that Guatemala was readying its armed forces for action. The possibility that General Arbenz would use Colonel Castillo's inadequately armed small band of exiles as an excuse for invasion, created considerable anxiety in both Honduras and El Salvador.

There may have been Intelligence that General Arbenz proposed invading Honduras and El Salvador with Soviet support in a drive southward towards the Panama Canal. If that were so, then it must have been in the realm of a future feasibility. The Panama Canal was quite distant from Guatemala, and its neighbours. But one factor gradually emerged; small though Guatemala was, its war-like preparations were not to be taken lightly. With Guatemala, in the heartland of Central America, a Communist bulwark, the malignancy could spread, endangering South as well as Central America.

For the United States a situation which had been grave but not dangerous began to assume a different character as the CIA's reports came in. General Arbenz was bringing the Guatemalan armed forces up to full combat strength. He needed modern weapons in great numbers, and it could be assumed that when he got them, he would move.

The US Defence Department and the CIA's mentor, the National Security Council, reviewed Intelligence estimates and summaries, and meanwhile, thousands of miles away, at the port city of Stettin in Communist Poland, a businessman who operated a steel and sheet-metal fabrication company, and whose hobby appeared to be watching ships arrive and depart through binoculars out of his office window, wrote a letter to a French company in which he gave full specifications concerning motor car parts which could be furnished cheaper than the competition could provide them. Like all letters leaving Eastern Bloc countries destined for delivery in the free countries, this message required a censor's approval. It was taken to the proper commissar, was duly stamped and was mailed.

The letter did not go directly to a French car-parts company, it went first to a CIA depository—or 'drop'—but from the 'drop' it was taken to a bona fide French car-parts company, whose director in turn took the letter to a photography studio at Montmartre where it was opened, photographed, then painstakingly examined until the microdot was discovered—under a 'period' at the end of a sentence—and the microdot was then carefully developed, enlarged and printed. It was a coded message. The agent who had done the developing was not a cryptologist. He was a microfilm expert, therefore, he could not read the code's message.

The enlarged, photographed microfilm message was then delivered to a radioman who transmitted it to Washington verbatim. He could not have deciphered it either.

In Washington the message was decoded by a cryptographic machine in the presence of the then-CIA director, Allen Welsh Dulles. It said that the freighter *Alfhem*, of Swedish registry, had taken on board at Stettin 15,000 wooden crates which had come overland from Czechoslovakia's Communist armament works of Skoda. CIA agents, other than the businessman at Stettin, were fairly certain this shipment of weaponry was destined for delivery somewhere in the Americas.

Agents in Europe were alerted to gather information on the

Alfhem. From Stockholm it was reported that the *Alfhem* belonged to the Swedish company of Angbats, A.B., which had placed the freighter under charter to the E. E. Dean agency in London.

From London it was reported that the E. E. Dean agency had rechartered the *Alfhem* to A. Christianson Company of Stockholm, and that the *Alfhem*'s manifests showed the vessel's hold was full of optical supplies and laboratory equipment destined to be delivered at Dakar in West Africa.

Shortly, then, agents in Africa reported to Washington that, more than two-thirds of the way to Dakar, the *Alfhem* had abruptly altered course and was now steaming towards the port of Trujillo in Honduras.

CIA specialists predicted what now ensued. The *Alfhem*, on course for Trujillo, abruptly altered course once more, and steamed directly for the Guatemalan harbour of Puerto Barrios, which was the best deep-water port nearest the Guatemalan-Honduran border on the Caribbean coast.

General Arbenz's troops and police blanketed the entire port facility to screen the *Alfhem*'s unloading. The crates were whisked away in covered trucks.

One day later, before the last of the crates had been opened and inventoried, CIA planners and analysts had the full list. The *Alfhem*'s cargo consisted of 2,000 tons of weaponry, ranging from artillery to small arms, plus ammunition. From this inventory, and based on General Arbenz's increasingly belligerent attitude, and also the fact that no armaments left the Skoda works without Soviet sanction, it was possible to arrive at an unpleasant conclusion: using Jacobo Arbenz Guzman, the Soviet Union proposed to secure a foothold in mainland Central America. If this occurred, and basing predictions on past Soviet performances, within a short length of time all Latin America, as well as the Caribbean community, would be under subversive attack.

The CIA's function had been to gather the information and produce a summary. Beyond that, a course of action would be the responsibility of others.

At a meeting of the Intelligence Advisory Committee, Allen Dulles presented the hard facts to the officers in charge of Intelligence for the armed services—army, navy, air force—as well as those representing the Joint Chiefs of Staff, the Federal Bureau of Investigation, the State Department, and the Atomic Energy Commission.

This meeting was followed by another one, this time with the National Security Council. Time was of course, critical. Intelligence from inside Guatemala implied that President Arbenz was preparing to move towards an armed confrontation with his neighbours.

Two days after the National Security Council met, on 17th May 1954, the US Secretary of State made a public announcement that the United States was aware of the arms shipment to Guatemala's Communist régime. From that point onward the Department of Defence took charge. An air lift to Colonel Castillo's Guatemalan partisans in exile provided the anti-Communists with sixty tons of weapons, equal in quality to anything Arbenz had received from the Soviets. Additionally, as Colonel Castillo's exiles grew in numbers, all armed with one machete, one burp gun, and one pistol, along with ample ammunition, 'someone' provided the Castillo forces with two vintage B-26 bombers.

What followed was predictable, even without CIA aid. Castillo Armas's exiles crossed out of Honduras into their homeland, and in the engagements which followed Arbenz's troops defected heavily. Also, as the exile 'air force' of two ancient B-26s soared over Guatemala City they were cheered from the ground. They dropped a few bombs, and Arbenz's air arm, three fast little P-38 fighter aircraft, also from World War II, joined the 'enemy'. The rest was a fiasco. The army declined to oppose the 'invaders', and even the Communist-controlled labour unions, which were expected to at least make a show of strength, declined to do so.

The Soviets did not sustain Arbenz, nor did they concede that they had had any hand in what had happened in Guatemala. Finally, Jacobo Arbenz Guzman fled the country. Subsequently, the point was that the CIA's effort was adequate and competent. The sequel to the story of Arbenz's ouster and his replacement by Castillo deserves mention elsewhere.

Colonel Castillo did not fulfil his promises of reform. Eventually, he appeared as a typical Central American autocrat, but that is a study for sociologists, perhaps even historians, and unfortunate as it may be, and regardless of accusations to the contrary, it was in no way the fault of the Central Intelligence Agency.

If there is an unfortunate aspect to supporting nationalists over Communists, it must lie in the fact that so many of the alternatives to Communist domination are not really very much better, only different.

As for the outcries of moralists that neither the CIA nor anyone else has a right to interfere in the politics of foreign lands, Cuba's outstanding lawyer, patriot and international observer, Mario Lazo, has noted that 'Intervention *per se* is not necessarily, or even usually, an evil thing. At times non-intervention is the greater evil. . . . Non-intervention in Cuba has meant . . . unilateral Soviet intervention. . . . It is indisputable that the United States cannot avoid involvement in the affairs of other nations. . . . When it gives economic aid it intervenes. When it withholds such aid . . . it intervenes.'

Nonetheless, it also is indisputable that in many places where US policy has employed CIA methods to defeat a Communist effort, as in Guatemala, and later in Iran, the alternatives have been neither commendable nor tidy.

Human nature being what it is, changes in government very often—in fact too often—result in the alternatives of a bastard or a son of a bitch. But human nature is not subject to CIA control, and even if it were, there is no reason to suspect, as in the case of Arbenz Guzman, that leaders who initially project one kind of image, will emerge differently once in power.

Perhaps if the articulators of condemnation were more pragmatic they would realize that politics is itself a spawning ground of vast numbers of amoral human beings, and that the CIA's efforts, when expended in an attempt to preserve or aid nationalism, cannot guarantee the choices subsequently offered voters. In Guatemala, to blame the Central Intelligence Agency for what followed the defeat of a Soviet conspiracy, was to overlook that Guatemalans had had their right to vote restored to them. What they subsequently did with that right was their affair.

A common criticism of the CIA has been, and continues to be, that the agency functions as the tool of a powerful reactionary (US) government whose intention has been to support repressive régimes, as opposed to popular movements seeking to bring about social justice.

The facts tend to disagree. In Guatemala, as in other lands, the

CIA, operating as directed, has supported the orderly processes, if they exist; if they do *not* exist, it supports their establishment, but beyond that the choices have belonged to the people, and whether or not Soviet or other expert disinformation has convinced people this is not so, all they must do to prove otherwise is to participate in one free election.

The Central Intelligence Agency does not establish policy. It operates in accordance with directives given it by US government leaders. It has been the free world's largest and most resourceful foil to the Soviet Union's all-powerful KGB. It has no representative at cabinet level. The KGB's director is a member of the Soviet *Politburo*. The CIA is prohibited from internal activity by law. The KGB supervises and monitors every aspect of Soviet life from art and literature to the operation of hospitals and nurseries. The CIA cannot unilaterally undertake an operation in a place such as Guatemala. The KGB can, without any authority beyond its own, arrest and execute Soviet citizens, have foreign leaders assassinated, and launch overt attacks in such places as Guatemala.

The Soviets subjugated Czechoslovakia in 1948 *in one day*. All its traditional techniques were observed in action, including KGB covert activity.

The CIA knew in advance that Soviet penetration of the Czech government had been in progress for some time. It also was aware that a third of the Czech Parliament were Soviet sympathizers and that in fact there were Communists in the cabinet.

When the blow fell Czechoslovakia was subjugated by a 'palace' *coup* which achieved success between breakfast and dinner. No troops were employed. Not a single shot was fired. A minority of Communists assumed power over a much greater majority of free Czechs.

Intervention could have preserved the freedom of Czechoslovakia. US policy-makers learned from the Czech example that intervention was the only alternative to the abandonment of small nations whose subjugation was otherwise inevitable.

The Soviet Union's methods of subversion followed by subjugation were perfected in the decade following World War II. The key was speed. As with Czechoslovakia, control was achieved before intervention was possible. Syria was penetrated, subverted, and yoked to Soviet ambition swiftly and successfully. Other nations lost their freedom the same way. The pattern seldom varied. In 1963 Nikita Khruschev said, 'Before World War II Communist parties existed in 43 countries. Today Communist parties exist in 90 [countries].'

In the 1970s, while professing détente, Communist forces subverted Chile, in Latin America, and made the attempt in Greece. In 1974, while soliciting 'favoured nation' status in trade agreements with the US, Soviet agents engineered the overthrow of Portugal's first democratic, free government in more than a generation.

It is possible that faith and trust will triumph, but indications suggest they will be unable to do so without aid, and if the efforts of the Central Intelligence Agency to secure men of great stature in positions of leadership, fail, as they unavoidably will, at least the fact that US policy favours free elections in all lands ensures for the people of those lands the opportunity to make changes.

Imperfect as this system may well be, the alternative of subversion followed by subjugation is far less attractive. The Hungarians learned how harsh that alternative was during the months of October and November 1956.

What has troubled many people in the past has been the feeling about ends justifying means. But a short-term discouragement, such as the Castillo Armas régime in Guatemala, must be considered in a perspective which regards it as a better alternative than long-term subjugation under a Soviet-supported Arbenz régime.

4

Coups and Croppers

In a recent book entitled *The CIA and the Cult of Intelligence*, there is a statement worthy of evaluation. It says, 'The loudly heralded Berlin tunnel operation of the mid-1950s—actually a large wiretap—provided tons of trivia and gossip, but provided little in the way of high-grade secret information that could be used by the agency's Intelligence analysts.'

As though in contradiction of this statement, at a meeting of the US government's official Discussion Group on Intelligence and Foreign Policy held on 8th January 1968, and attended by both CIA officials and unaffiliated members who constituted a cross-section of the US establishment, it was said that while clandestine penetration (ordinary espionage) has not been wholly successful in closed societies such as the Soviet Union, there have been 'brilliant successes (like the Berlin tunnel) . . .'.

In the face of such opposite conclusions, inevitably speculation arose as to what the truth might be. No answer was ever offered by the CIA, the executive branch of the government, or the US State Department. Nonetheless, in vignette form, the facts are as follows.

In the summer of 1954 four East German businessmen held a conference in Berlin which lasted several hours, and subsequently one of these men returned to his home with what appeared to be a standard business contract. He subsequently forwarded this contract to a French businessman at Marseilles.

All of these men were CIA agents. The business contract they had so meticulously drafted was a series of detailed instructions which revealed the location of an underground juncture of telephone cables which handled the official calls of East Germany's civil authorities, and the calls of East Germany's Soviet overlords. These cables were capable of accommodating more than four hundred simultaneous communications, both incoming and outgoing, to and from all parts of the world.

The 'business contract' was ultimately delivered to CIA headquarters, at that time located in Washington, where it was decoded and became a prime issue at several executive CIA conferences.

Subsequently, orders were sent forth for a physical verification to be made, and although it required a considerable delay before the hole was dug and the exact location of the juncture could be verified—a clandestine crew could not simply go forth in Communist East Germany and start digging—eventually the verification report was sent to Washington giving the specifications. The juncture was five feet below the ground, beneath the East German village of Alt-Glienicke, which was located approximately 2,000 feet from the West German village of Rudow, in the American Zone.

On the East German side there was an *autobahn* of arterial importance, heavily travelled, particularly by East German and Soviet border patrols. Also, there was an aerodrome between the location of the juncture and the *autobahn*— Schoenfeld Airport.

The objective being to tap, tape, and monitor all conversations going forth and being received on those four-hundred-odd communication cables, round the clock, it was not feasible to dig down on the Communist side, splice in all the bulky, very technical electronics equipment, nor create plausible excuses for technicians to be nearby in large numbers; therefore it was decided to tunnel from Rudow in the US Zone, under the border, beneath the *autobahn*, the airport and the East German village of Alt-Glienicke, to the location of the juncture.

Accordingly, in the late summer of 1954, preparations were made. First, a US Air Force radar facility was constructed, complete with all the visible, external impedimenta of such an installation—all of it under binocular observation from East Germany. Barracks, watch-towers, scanning aerials, garages, offices, workshops, were all constructed. The facility was genuine in every way. Inside the buildings the excavating was begun.

The earth which was removed was crated, labelled as electronics equipment and hauled away. The tunnel was taken down to a depth of twenty feet, on an incline, and pushed beyond the border, beneath the *autobahn*, in the desired direction, under

Schoenfeld Airport, towards the village of Alt-Glienicke.

The work progressed well, but slowly. Every precaution against detection was observed. By late autumn, when the tunnel was nearing completion, and it became cold enough to hamper digging, large heaters were installed.

The tunnel was beneath the airport when monitoring devices detected the sound of digging above. At once all work ceased, the excavation crews were withdrawn back to the US Zone, and instructions were passed to an agent in the Communist Zone to investigate. It was learned that a labour gang was replacing faulty water pipes, and that their trench would only reach to a depth of several feet.

The excavating was resumed, and in due course the tunnel was pushed to the site of the underground communication lines. The excavators were withdrawn and the electronics specialists were sent in.

The tunnel was six feet in diameter and was walled with precision-fitted steel panels. It had pumps to carry off seepage-water, was well lighted and adequately heated. In fact it was so well heated that the entire undertaking nearly came to disaster when a light snowfall covered all the countryside—except the arrow-straight course of the tunnel where heat rising up through the ground melted snow as fast as it fell.

A horrified sentry at one of the radar installation watchtowers hastened to report the existence of this tell-tale snowless pathway, and all heat was immediately turned off in the tunnel, a refrigerant system was hurriedly rushed in and shortly afterwards the falling snow began to stick.

Telephone switchboards were installed, as well as electrical boosters to maintain the energy level at all times. Electronics specialists spliced into all the lines without allowing even a one-second interruption, and amplifying units were installed which permitted energy impulses to remain absolutely normal while every communication, incoming as well as outgoing, was routed through recording units back at the radar facility.

US intelligence specialists monitored East German and Soviet conversations, evaluated orders from Moscow, learned code-names of Communist secret agents, some operating in West Germany, were privy to Soviet and East German disagreements, collected and catalogued a vast list of names of officials, along with considerable personal data on most of them, and for close to a year were able to listen to Soviet plans for harassment of the Allied sectors, in advance.

Also, they collected an enormous amount of trivia, as the authors of *The CIA and the Cult of Intelligence* alleged, but even banalities have value.

Finally, in late April of 1956, some Soviet signal corps troops inadvertently discovered the tunnel. It was abandoned at once. By the time the Soviets broke through, the tunnel had served its purpose. *Not a single Communist telephone communication into or out of East Germany during a critical period in East-West relations had not been recorded.*

Former CIA chief Allen Dulles once said, 'Most Intelligence operations have a limited span of usefulness.' This applied to the Berlin tunnel; while it remained operational it certainly lived up to expectations.

There was a sequel, of course. The Soviet government sent a protest to Washington calling for disciplinary action against those involved in 'subterranean espionage', and the Soviet press denounced the tunnel as a violation of the 'sovereign rights of the German Democratic Republic', overlooking the fact that the Soviet troops who discovered the tunnel, a small segment of a much more formidable array of Soviet force, was an even greater violation of German sovereignty.

The final footnote was made possible when the Soviets opened the tunnel to the German public in order that East Germans could see how the perfidious Americans operated. The results were unique. Instead of being outraged, the Germans thought it was very funny that the Americans had listened to Soviet conversations, undetected, for a year. The Soviets then closed the tunnel to the public on 9th June 1956.

The tunnel was a success, but two years after it was officially closed by the Soviets, in 1958, the agency became involved in another affair which was anything but a success. It involved an area of the world where stability has never been notable, and where currently nations and leaders are heavily engaged in a petroleum confrontation.

Specifically, this area is bounded northward by the Caspian Sea, southward by the Red Sea, and utilizes as its sea arteries both the Atlantic and Indian Oceans, which support its lifelines via the Mediterranean Sea and the Persian Gulf.

It constitutes a region of relatively small, weak, and agriculturally unendowed nations, which, except for what lies below the surface of these lands—oil in enormous amounts—would relegate them to a very minor role. But because of the oil derived from these lands, without which the highly industrialized Western nations could not continue to maintain their economic health and rate of growth, Western politicians, statesmen, and Intelligence communities have had a keen interest in them, and that makes what ensues even more of a CIA embarrassment.

In these sheikhdoms, emirates and kingdoms seething with rivalries, jealousies, and all manner of factionalism, the CIA was of necessity well represented. It owned outright a number of highly placed politicians, and also had its special secret agents well positioned. For example, when it learned of a plot to assassinate King Hussein of Jordan, it moved at once to aid in the identification of the plotters—army men—so that Hussein could take appropriate steps.

Elsewhere, little Kuwait, with an estimated twenty per cent of all known oil reserves and a population of less than half a million people, lying at the upper, inland, end of the Persian Gulf, a British protectorate for sixty years, was beginning to anticipate full sovereignty with a suspected leaning towards leftism. It was considered essential in the West that the oil emirates be kept free of Communism, or even moderate leftism. The industrialized West could not allow one of its major petroleum suppliers to fall into unfriendly hands.

The CIA was actively interested in Kuwaiti politics, too. Jordan and Kuwait were strategically important communities. It could have been anticipated that the CIA would affect as agreeable a resolution of difficulties in Kuwait as it had managed in Jordan.

It probably would have, too, but while the CIA was looking both ways, towards Jordan and Kuwait, the explosion occurred in between, in Iraq, where there had been almost no indication of trouble. Not only the CIA was caught unprepared. On 14th July 1958, at five o'clock in the morning, elements of the Iraqi army—the Twentieth Brigade, among other units—quietly surrounded the Royal Palace at Baghdad, while King Faisal, cousin to Jordan's King Hussein, was shaving. Neither Faisal, his uncle, Crown Prince Abdul Illah, nor Premier Nuri es Said, had any inkling a revolution was coming.

Orders were sent into the palace for the immediate surrender of King Faisal. Instead of complying Faisal and Crown Prince Abdul Illah appeared at palace windows, guns in hand, and opened fire. In retaliation the Iraqi army blasted the palace with artillery, setting it on fire.

King Faisal, the Crown Prince, the royal family along with several retainers, abandoned the palace by a rear exit, and were confronted by insurgent troops. Within minutes King Faisal, Crown Prince Abdul Illah, his two sisters, and mother were shot to death. There were a few additional casualties. Abdul Illah's corpse was torn to pieces by an aroused mob, and Premier Nuri es Said, in hiding, was sold to the army by a retainer, and when apprehended, after a fierce fight, was shot to death, torn apart, and his remnants were dragged through the streets of Baghdad.

Several foreigners, including Colonel P. L. Graham of the British Embassy, and an American, Eugene Burns, of California, were also killed by mobs, largely led by KGB infiltrators and terrorists.

The upheaval was finished, almost before it was known to have erupted, in such places as London and Washington.

The Americans could not immediately identify the *coup*'s leader, an Iraqi brigadier-general named Abdul Karim el-Kassem, although the British, who had been in the Persian Gulf area since before the turn of the present century, knew Karim as a leftist officer in command of the Iraqi army's Twentieth Brigade.

When the surprise passed, it was asked how this *coup* could have occurred, and the answer was simply that although there *had* been some rumours, questionable ones of the kind to be heard every day in the Middle East, as elsewhere, there had been no hard Intelligence to the effect that anything serious was imminent in Iraq.

To the question : how could this be, when a strong element of the Iraqi army had been involved, the answer was that the troops participating had been authorized to pass through Baghdad the night of 13th July, on their way to join other elements of the Iraqi army then serving in Jordan. General Kassem's Twentieth Brigade, in full combat panoply, was joined in Baghdad that night by other elements of the Iraqi army, by order of General Kassem, who seemed to have decided to inaugurate his *coup* only a few hours before ordering Faisal's palace surrounded.

The first inkling foreigners had that there had been a *coup* occurred shortly after Faisal's death when Radio Baghdad, prefaced its programmes by announcing : 'This is Radio Baghdad in the Republic of Iraq.'

Kassem's strategy succeeded, obviously, because, while he was in contact with other Iraqi dissidents, whom he asked to join him in Baghdad on the night of 13th July, it was not generally known nor suspected that his *coup* was to take place on 14th July. Lt General Rafiq Aref, Chief of Staff of the Iraqi army, was taken as much by surprise as was King Faisal, and the CIA. Aref was taken into custody on 14th July.

The excitement which followed Kassem's *coup* resulted in the burning of the British Embassy, in attacks upon suspected CIA agents, and violent demonstrations at the US Embassy, but these events were anti-climactic. Abdul Karim el-Kassem was the master of Iraq, a leftist with pronounced anti-British, anti-American tendencies, when the US and the CIA had been confident that Iraq, as a pro-West member of the Baghdad Pact, was safe from either Soviet influence or internal dissidence.

Slightly more than a week after Faisal's death, the Foreign Relations Committee of the US Senate undertook a probe to ascertain why the CIA, with ample funds and agents, as well as listening posts throughout the Middle East, had been caught so completely unprepared. Although it was said no one had even suspected such a *coup* was possible, the CIA *did* know it was a possibility.

In the *coup* which was supposed to follow the assassination of Jordan's King Hussein, discovered and promptly thwarted in Jordan one week before the Iraqi *coup*, a number of the captured plotters told of a *coup* destined to take place shortly in Iraq. The CIA said it had forwarded this information to the British, as well as to King Faisal's Iraqi government.

Also, the CIA had learned through local sources in the US that some variety of plot was in progess in Iraq but it did not, in either case, that of the captives in Jordan or the local source in the US, make an investigation.

Even so, the results might not have been insurmountable, until, in the summer of 1961, Kassem followed Britain's relinquishment of protective (or proprietory) rights in Kuwait by claiming Kuwait as part of Iraq. By that time there was no longer speculation concerning Kassem's leftism. He had appeared as an open advocate of legitimizing the Communist party in Iraq, his chief bureaucrats in several strategic government posts were known Communists, he had renounced the pro-Western Baghdad Pact, and had taken Iraq out of the alliance with pro-Western Jordan.

In 1961 Britain derived at least fifty per cent of its essential petroleum imports from the areas contiguous to the Persian Gulf, forty per cent coming from threatened Kuwait.

When Kassem made his announcement concerning annexation of Kuwait, and alerted his tough, capable army, 60,000 strong, Britain sent 4,000 troops to Kuwait, where the Kuwaiti armed forces, 2,400 strong, were placed on a war footing.

The defiance which Kassem's announcement brought forth from many concerned sources, including some in the Arab world such as Egypt which offered armed aid to Kuwait, caused Iraq's government to retreat from its intransigent position. Although this particular threat passed, when the CIA was caught *sans culottes* in 1958 by the Iraqi rebellion, the good-will of a strategic Middle Eastern nation situated in the heartland of the oil emirates was lost to the West. The full cost of that loss to the West was not to be felt for about sixteen years, or until the oil-exporting nations encouraged by Kassem, in emulation of his example, joined together to blackmail the industrial West, threatening to provoke a world-wide depression through deprivation of oil, and also by astronomically increasing oil prices, although in 1958 only a few astute observers, and none at the media level, envisaged any such possibility.

The real value of the Intelligence-gathering function has always been to anticipate and insofar as it is possible to thwart future dangers. This fact has been demonstrated time and again by failures, as in the case of Iraq. But it is only recognizable when a failure occurs. When success obtains, no one can actually say what the cost of failure would have been. They can predicate, on the basis of possibilities, trends and probable motivations, but since the overthrow of a government was not allowed to happen, it cannot factually be said what would have occurred if a *coup* had succeeded, and because of this, it has always been easy, and often politically expedient, to denounce a CIA success as loudly as it has been to denounce a CIA failure.

In Iraq, if the CIA had anticipated Kassem's *coup* and had thwarted it, the denunciations would have been equally as vituperative as they were over the CIA's failure, but they would instead have been based upon hurled charges of interfering in the affairs of another nation, rather than the fact that the CIA had *failed* to interfere.

It is charmingly altruistic to denounce Intelligent operations in foreign lands on humanitarian and ethical grounds, but sadly, perhaps, altruism supplies no oil, protects no vital interests, and never air-lifts enough food.

As in the Chilean affair of 1970 (Chapter Five), as, in fact, in most of the secret wars engaged in worldwide between the KGB and the CIA, it might be well for those whose lamentations and denunciations are the loudest to reflect upon the probability that as long as these two organizations to a considerable extent checkmate one another in their campaigns of 'dirty tricks', subversion, infiltration, candid bribery and terrorism, the armies, with the arsenals, of their sponsoring countries will not march.

Quite possibly *détente* is not a game of statesmanship, as many believe, but is a result of basic, realistic, and unappetizing politics which has less to do with trade and cultural agreements than it has to do with a checkmate between Soviet and United States Intelligence, both of whom are motivated by the requirements of an environment where strategic politics, without altruism, idealism, or very much ethical decency, unequivocally exists.

5

The Chilean Affiliation

In April of 1961 the United States achieved an historic political blunder when it deliberately withheld armed support for the invading forces of free Cuba, which it had painstakingly and expensively trained to destroy Fidel Castrol's Communist government, and by a stab in the back doomed those men to death and capture.

The result was history's infamous Bay of Pigs disaster, reaffirmation of Fidel Castro's repressive rule in Cuba, and a black day in US history (see Chapter Six), which to a considerable extent during the ensuing years troubled the United States public and political consciences even though apologists insisted that since Cuba was separate from mainland America, and therefore susceptible to United States surround, blockade and containment, the damage was negligible.

Whether these claims were true or not remained to be seen, but an outgrowth of the United States failure to support those men, and also to support the 138-year-old Monroe Doctrine which opposed establishment of foreign power in the Western Hemisphere, was a fresh conviction among United States leaders that a reoccurrence must not be permitted, and as a result of this posture, when a second Soviet-sponsored thrust was made, this time on the Latin American mainland, in strategic Chile, the United States reacted swiftly, fiercely, and not very tidily, creating a scandal whose reverberations are still felt.

The Chilean affair has been termed an over-reaction resulting from the Cuban *fait accompli*, which it may very well be. Nevertheless, what happened in Chile was an excellent example of how national leaders reasoning from political motivations, and an Intelligence community which is subservient to political authority, and susceptible to the requirements of politicians who, in turn, are dependent on Big Money for political support, become involved in situations which, at best, are not attractive, and which ultimately become epitomes of duplicity and ugliness.

Chile, a coastal nation of South America with a population of ten million people, had a national election slated for September of 1970, with one of the presidential aspirants a man of avowed Marxist sentiments, Salvador Allende Gossens, considered an almost certain victor.

United States Intelligence reports had confirmed what other sources including the United States State Department already suspected: that Salvador Allende favoured expropriation of foreign investments, confiscation of foreign-owned or controlled properties, and the establishment in Chile of a sanctuary for Cuban, European, Middle-Eastern and American leftist-terrorists.

It would have been difficult to find a man whose political platform was less acceptable to United States and European interests in all Latin America, and yet Salvador Allende was in fact a paradoxical Marxist.

For example, he believed he could achieve a blend of Communism and democracy. He favoured individual wealth, good living, scorned the traditional beard, weaponry and fatigue uniform of Cuba's *Fidelistas*, did not wear a beret, and scolded students for plotting revolutions when they were supposed to be studying.

He chose not to fraternize with the poor people, from whom he derived most of his support, lived very well, was anything but a political fanatic, and was a likable, kindly man of considerable charm and incredibly naïve political beliefs, and although his friend Fidel Castro had told him that the only successful way to make a revolution was with guns, Allende, a fastidious man, well groomed and by nature orderly, who did not really like violence, was convinced his unique variety of 'democratic Communism' through persuasion, fiscal manipulation, personal charm, and USSR support, could succeed without guns.

At the outset of Allende's political career only one of these attributes appeared reliable, and near the close of his political career, when serious confrontation came, that source of comfort to Allende—the USSR—withdrew.

The man, Salvador Allende, was improbable enough. The situation in South America during and immediately prior to his

The seal of the CIA

Allen Dulles, director of the CIA from 1953 to 1961 and the longest-serving chief to date

tenure as Chilean chief executive, was even more unique. What had for years been a United States preserve, protectorate, or proprietary, had been alarmingly infiltrated by anti-United States leftists, mostly Cuban exports. United States influence was being increasingly challenged as never before. Latin America, the vulnerable underbelly of United States security, was being dangerously subverted.

Cuba, with strong Soviet support, had been tirelessly exporting terrorism to mainland Latin America for a decade. Saboteurs, assassins, propagandists, professional infiltrators and terrorist organizers, had successfully created Communist organizations in Panama, Costa Rica, Honduras, Peru, Ecuador, Mexico, and Chile, and it had to be against this background of growing opposition to the United States that subsequent events in Chile were viewed.

Clearly, the Soviets, through their off-shore satellite Cuba, were in process of perfecting a nation-by-nation secret and silent conquest of Latin America. In Uruguay the Tupamaro movement was flourishing. In Mexico a secret scheme to completely control the nation was being perfected. (One year later, in 1971, this plan was to culminate in an incredible plot which very nearly succeeded.)

Communist agents were in the cities, the *barrios*, the mountains, the labour unions, and eventually in the governments of all Latin American nations.

By 1970, with violent challenge to several governments, as in Uruguay, scheduled, a mainland sanctuary was needed. Salvador Allende was the best hope of the Communists in South America. His strategically valuable homeland, Chile, could provide a haven, and Allende could provide a legal protector, providing Allende won the national presidential election in September 1970.

Chile, with the longest coastline on the eastern South American seaboard, was an ideal staging area for an ultimate conquest of Argentina, as well as that largest of all American sovereignties, Brazil. Additionally, Chile offered access to Peru, Colombia, and, adjacent to Colombia, that flourishing, oil-rich back door to the Caribbean—Red Cuba's private lake—Venezuela.

Without doubt, the Americas were vulnerable. The United States, its continental under-belly a target for Soviet infiltration and subversion for over a generation, had until recent times managed to prevent serious threats from the south, but the establishment of Communist Cuba off-shore of both North and South America in 1961 had apparently ensured what had occurred in mainland Latin America in 1970: the first real crisis-condition for the United States in over a century; a situation which, if it were not neutralized, could very well have brought America's leaders face to face with something no one had envisaged in many lifetimes: foreign conquest.

This was the condition in the Western Hemisphere at the time of Salvador Allende's bid for presidential power in Chile. That this crisis-condition existed was recognized in Moscow, Washington, and Havana. Elsewhere in the world there was very little knowledge and even less interest in what was happening, or what *might* happen, in Latin America.

For the United States the situation was critical. Uruguay's government was in danger of succumbing to the Communist Tupamaro guerrillas. In the Argentine, Peru, Colombia, even in Guatemala where the abortive Arbenz Guzman affair of 1954 had taught patience to zealous dissidents, failure on the part of intimidated supporters of free nationalism to halt the Communist thrust had encouraged the virulent spread of the most dangerous variety of hemispherical anti-Americanism the United States had ever faced, and not one United States citizen out of hundreds had any inkling such a condition existed. Secret wars of the kind the Intelligence communities engage in, are fought this way, in a vacuum. Czechoslovakia, conquered in *one day*, was an example.

Later, it was a simple thing for the derogators of United States intervention in Chile to vilify the government and its intervention instrument, the Central Intelligence Agency, while avoiding the redundant question of what the cost of non-intervention might have been.

Nevertheless, despite the fact that the United States sent in teams of agents to distribute over a million dollars among Chile's politicians and labour leaders, for the purpose of influencing voters against Salvador Allende, it was a case of too little, too late. The Communists had been in Chile longer, had expertly cultivated the same people, and had diligently applied their rather considerable expertise to ensure Allende's triumph in the September 1970 national elections.

Even so, Allende's victory was achieved by a slim majority.

So small a majority in fact that this 'new epoch' of 'meat pies and red wine' would in all probability not have been able to survive its first crisis, without Soviet support.

In most Latin American countries where rightist army cliques exert a hawkish vigil over civilian politics and react instantly at sight of the first red flag, Salvador Allende would not have been inaugurated. In Chile, where the traditional separation of civil government and the armed services has always been strong, the rightist generals and admirals did nothing.

The secret war began when Allende was installed as chief executive in Santiago's Moneda Palace, residence of Chilean presidents. The United States, through local rightists and Central Intelligence Agency personnel began simultaneously to undermine both Allende and the Chilean economy. Five million dollars was spent where it would promote labour disputes, newspaper attacks upon the president, sabotage, fuel and food shortages. That was the beginning. Over the ensuing three years, beginning with Allende's inauguration in September of 1970, the United States, through its Central Intelligence Agency, spent a minimum of $8,000,000 to bring down Chile's Marxist government.

Outside the sphere of the Central Intelligence Agency the United States government exerted pressure through the sources of grants and credits. The Export Import Bank denied Chile's request for a loan, and purchasers of Chile's produce cut back or cancelled their delivery requirements.

On the other side, the Communist élite did as it had done before in direct confrontations; it contributed a never-failing supply of emotional and bombastic rhetoric, small arms, tons of pamphlets designed to inflame the populace, a little money, some expendable leadership, and avoided anything which could have proved as humiliating as the Cuban missile confrontation of a decade earlier.

The Central Intelligence Agency had its agents in strategic locations throughout Chile. 'In place' spies, hired informers, and those whose ideological opposition to Allende and Marxism made them valuable—some in Allende's government, and also in the army—aided the process of attrition.

Taxi drivers, newsmen, storekeepers, dock-workers, labour officials, policemen, served the CIA as spies, informers and agents. The move to bring down South America's first freely elected Marxist president was resolute, well funded and, up to a point, it epitomized the sequences followed by professional subverters.

It succeeded, but it might better have done so if several giant United States conglomerates such as the International Telephone and Telegraph Corporation (ITT) and Anaconda Copper Company had not, at first, become rivals of the CIA in Chile, and subsequently, associates of the CIA.

ITT's enmity towards Allende stemmed from the president's policies of expropriation. ITT was not the only United States corporation with investments to protect in Chile, but it certainly was one of the richest, with 'surface assets' (visible holdings, as opposed to subsidiary or unaffiliated assets acquired through ITT investment funds) worth $150,000,000.

As early as the spring of 1970, before the Chilean elections, but not before Allende's expropriation plans became known, ITT's directors began their own campaign of attrition by granting funds to Allende's political rivals for the presidency. ITT also undertook a vigorous lobbying campaign in the United States to influence national leaders, and this was more successful, although, as the Chilean elections of 1970 came closer, opposition to the establishment of another Communist government in the hemisphere had more than enough opposition in the Congress and the White House.

In terms of money spent, the CIA's $8,000,000 was not impressive in comparison to similar efforts in other countries, but Chile was not a large, rich, or strong nation. Also, the CIA's $8,000,000 was in addition to the millions spent by ITT and the other large United States corporations with Chilean investments, and finally, when the Chilean Congress confirmed Salvador Allende as President, and the real effort to destroy him began, the United States conglomerates loosened their purse strings still more, the alternatives being as they were.

ITT, which was aware of the CIA's efforts in Chile, in a series of secret meetings with CIA officials offered to co-ordinate ITT's plans of subversion with those of the Central Intelligence Agency, and the CIA declined.

Subsequently, though, at another meeting, arranged this time through even more secret channels, ITT representatives met with Wilson V. Broe, at this time Chief of the Western Hemisphere Division of Clandestine Services, the CIA's top Latin American espionage specialist, and were informed that the CIA *would* co-operate, to the extent of providing leadership for the joint effort, as well as the joint funding.

Between these meetings, at a conference undoubtedly held at the White House, the Executive Branch of the United States government, the CIA's command authority, (President Richard Nixon) had performed a *volte face*.

President Nixon's national security advisor, Henry Kissinger, was known to oppose Communist entrenchment anywhere in the Western Hemisphere, after Cuba, on the grounds of spreading contamination, and, with Richard Nixon, already in 1970, sensitive to the rumblings within his personal political sphere, United States foreign policy was being single-handedly formulated and supervised by Dr Kissinger. Subsequently, he was to say, 'The CIA had nothing to do with the *coup* . . .' which brought Allende down in 1973, but in 1970 he had listened to the proposal of an ITT-CIA effort against the Allende régime, and as assistant to the President for National Security, had approved it.

Another official, a former Assistant Secretary of State, Charles Meyer, further buttressed the untruths with a statement to the effect that in the Allende matter the United States had 'bought no votes, . . . funded no candidates . . . [and] . . . promoted no *coups*'.

For the consumption of the United States public which was generally ignorant of what was in progress in Latin America, and in Chile specifically, others including a Deputy Assistant Secretary of State named Harry Schlaudeman, offered denials of United States implication with bland and believable untruths. Schlaudeman said, 'The United States Government adhered to a policy of non-intervention in Chile's internal affairs during the Allende period.' Even the United States President, Richard Nixon, in his most ambiguously pious Billy Grahamese said that 'As far as what happened in Chile is concerned, we can only say that for the United States to have intervened in a free election and to have turned it around, I think would have had repercussions all around Latin America that would have been far worse than what happened in Chile.'

Hypocrisy, during Allende's reign and later, simply made an unfortunate affair look worse, and the association of the Central Intelligence Agency with ITT and other United States private companies with interests to protect in Chile, additionally damaged

United States and CIA prestige. It also presented leftists the world over with a golden opportunity to 'prove' that the CIA did not really serve the interests of Western security, it served the giant capitalist conglomerates.

Undeniably, in Chile the CIA formed an alliance with Big Money. As for the announcement that the agency had no hand in the *coup* which ultimately brought down Marxist Allende, even had it been true—which it was not—that was the same as saying that although the French Revolution brought Louis XVI to the guillotine in 1793, the functionary who beheaded Louis was responsible for his death, not the Revolution or the Jacobins.

The destruction of Salvador Allende and his inept régime was orchestrated from beginning to end by the Central Intelligence Agency, affiliated with several giant United States business concerns. It was accomplished competently and satisfactorily, in the traditional manner, which means that in small nations of limited resources the key to chaos is economics. Especially in a nation such as Chile, where the armed services remained aloof and there were already cracks in the fiscal structure.

Chile was in financial difficulties before Allende became president. In fact, it was because of this condition, and Allende's promise to correct it, that he narrowly won the election.

The nation had long been one of the most stable democracies in Latin America. Its fiscal policies were sound, its currency, the *escudo*, was respected in world money markets, its laws were fair, enlightened and equitable, while its traditions were generally nationalistic and conservative. *But*, as elsewhere, the frugal land had of late been required to support a steadily increasing population, and over the past generation or so there had been a decline in production, exports, and foreign exchange.

Nitrate, at one time Chile's most reliable export, succumbed to synthetic production. Neither copper, another export commodity of value, nor a recently developed wine industry could carry the entire financial load, although they and other Chilean innovations had helped to sustain the national credit, as well as the slender reserve of foreign exchange.

But Chile's economy was frail and ailing when the Allende crisis appeared, a condition United States economists knew very well. Accordingly, CIA efforts to create havoc faced no serious obstacles. In a hand-to-mouth economy one transport strike brought hunger to the cities, one dock-side labour dispute created critical fuel shortages. A denial of credit by the Export-Import Bank in Washington created panic in Chilean ministries. The West, including the United States, got its own taste of this variety of real politics after Allende was gone, in 1974, when the oil emirates halted all petroleum shipments to the industrial nations. The difference was that in Chile the peril extended to all areas of the economy, not just petroleum.

Finally, a valuable although unwilling ally of the CIA-ITT coalition was the President himself. Allende's incredible ineptness hastened the inevitable. He insisted that storekeepers sell at less than cost. He advocated unsupported paper currency, and a wildly spiralling inflation followed. He nationalized the very modern and efficient Chilean agricultural system, and it broke down in complete confusion. Finally, with his constituents becoming increasingly disillusioned, he turned more and more to the leftist terrorists he had encouraged to settle in Chile, and who were already cordially despised by the Chileans.

He could not have survived *if* he had not been assured of outside leftist support. It was this *if* which prompted the CIA finally to court the generals and admirals. Experience, gained in part by observation of how Czechoslovakia had been subjugated in one day, prompted the CIA's quiet encouragement of a military *coup,* an event as alien to the Chilean social structure as it was commonplace among Chile's neighbours. (Bolivia to the north, for example, has had 189 national uprisings in the past 146 years.)

By October of 1972 when Allende had been in office for thirteen months, conditions were bad enough for the tearful chief executive to say that his country was 'on the verge of civil war'.

He was correct, although a *coup* was much more probable, even though Chile's apolitical generals, while adamantly opposed to Marxism, were still, in the autumn of 1972, reluctant to break with tradition. But by 1973 the national economy was in such a shambles, terrorists were so increasingly infiltrating the country, Communist agitators, mainly from Cuba, were so outspokenly hopeful of Chile's internal collapse, that the military finally appeared to itself—and the CIA—as Chile's last hope for survival.

Nevertheless, the crisis limped along another eleven months, with the nation sinking deeper into an economic and social morass, while Salvador Allende, drinking heavily, becoming more confused—and more pathetically ludicrous as he took to carrying a pistol and wearing a (US-style) helmet—shrilly refused demands for his resignation.

Now, the CIA stood clear of the crumbling structure, able finally to adopt the 'observation status' it had been claiming as its role; the momentum would do the rest.

And it did.

When the junta struck, it announced that the armed services were engaging in a crusade to 'fight for the liberation of the fatherland from the Marxist yoke'. Simultaneously the borders were closed, foreigners were warned away, communication with the outside world was suspended, and the attack which was launched against Allende, forted up in Moneda Palace with a few armed supporters, was pressed vigorously with troops, tanks, and warplanes.

Elsewhere in Santiago leftist gunmen were caught atop buildings by armed helicopters, terrorists and agitators were hunted by troops, Communist officials of the Allende régime were captured, or killed, on sight, the prisons were filled and the slain were hauled away in army vehicles.

Salvador Allende, sixty-five years old in 1973, died early in the violence. The official communiqué said he had committed suicide but those who saw the body before it was wrapped in a poncho and speedily removed from Moneda Palace by troops, marvelled that a man could shoot himself so many times before expiring.

The junta continued its work with, what was for Chile, unprecedented fury. While Salvador Allende was being buried at Viña del Mar, without spectators or mourners, *Operación Limpieza*, the 'clean-up' continued, and leftists in Europe, the United States and of course Havana and Moscow, cried out against the excesses, of which there were many, but their lamentations over the loss of their Chilean sanctuary were much louder.

In the US press, where the extent of CIA complicity was not generally known at the time of Allende's fall (as compared to the Santiago press where it *was* known, long before the fall), many writers were able to overlook Allende's mistakes and lament only the establishment of another Latin American military dictatorship.

For the general public a number of harrowing tales were told to foster proper indignation, including one concerning a woman alternatively known as Fitzgerald or Conger. She was allegedly threatened with rape by Chilean soldiers, was compelled to appear partially naked in the streets, was repeatedly struck and abused by troops, and was vilely tortured.

Amy Conger was a US national engaged in covert subversion for leftists while in Chile, a fact subsequently verified by US consular officials in Santiago. She was not tortured or threatened, although she was roughly handled when taken into custody by troops. She was released from custody at the request of the US consul and returned to the US, where her lurid story made excellent newspaper copy.

However, the Conger episode was not an isolated instance. Stories of cruelty and injustice repeatedly surfaced for months after the fall of Salvador Allende. Some were true, many were fabrications, but in either case they influenced public—and Congressional—opinion, and eventually, when the true extent of CIA involvement in Chile became known, the indignation was considerable and nationwide.

What seemed to harm the CIA's image most was that the agency had, in league with billion-dollar business conglomerates, performed capitalism's dirty work, and that a US President, his to-be Secretary of State, and other high government officials had lied about it.

(An unrelated and probably insignificant historical footnote to the Allende matter was that Salvador Allende was in the final stages of a terminal heart ailment when he was killed.)

6

The Real Bay of Pigs

There surely must be a political axiom which suggests how impossible it would be for a small nation existing beside a large and powerful nation to avoid being unduly influenced by its big neighbour.

In alliance with the powerful nation, it could probably be expected that the small nation would be a reflection of the large nation's policies and if it were to oppose the large nation it could be expected that the small nation would exist in a shadow of uncertainty and fear.

Cuba, which is ninety miles offshore from the United States, is such a small nation. In the decade immediately preceding the turn of the present century, when the US warned Spain against reinforcing Spanish garrisons in the Caribbean, little Cuba hurled an echoing denunciation. In 1914 when the United States warned Germany against any hemispherical intrusions, Cuba echoed that sentiment, and when the United States again warned Germany, and her Axis allies, in 1939, little Cuba made military and naval bases available to the United States.

Small nations, it appeared, could not be truly independent of their nearest most powerful neighbours. Then, in the late 1950s this seemed to no longer be true, and by the 1960s even the big powerful neighbour had to concede that it was not true, when little Cuba sanctioned the establishment upon its island of a Soviet-supported Communist satrapy, ninety miles offshore of democracy's bastion, the United States of America.

How this occurred is a story of United States weakness in leadership, illogical vacillation, and downright betrayal by Washington, but in that matter the Central Intelligence Agency's role was insignificant. The indisputable fact was that by 1959, a terrorist, an economic madman, a political dupe named Fidel Castro, was the master of Cuba.

By 1960 his United States admirers were becoming disillusioned. By 1961 when Castro's virulent anti-Americanism was no longer a secret, and the United States had the hard facts, brought to light largely through an investigation by a Senate Internal Security sub-committee, the damage had been so well done that there was no way of diplomatically undoing it.

Procrastination ensued and was abetted by continuing weak and vacillating United States leadership which deliberately did nothing, even though United States feeling towards Cuba was hardening. What either prompted, or at least encouraged, that procrastination was a series of events elsewhere in the world which seemed, on the surface at any rate, to be unrelated to Cuba, while appearing directly to imperil United States interests everywhere else.

Soviet threats against West Berlin were augmented by ominous shifts of USSR armed might. World disarmament hopes were destroyed by the truculent tirades of then-Premier Nikita Khrushchev's denunciations of what he termed 'interference' by Western militarist forces, and in May, there occurred the U2 spyplane incident, which was used utterly to shatter the Summit peace negotiations.

Finally, in abrupt succession there came a series of unsettling events including insurgency in Rhodesia, bloody and crippling riots in Japan, a political explosion in the Congo and finally the announcement by Premier Khrushchev that in the western hemisphere the Monroe Doctrine was unenforceable, and if the United States moved against Red Cuba the Soviet Union would retaliate by bombing US bases in Europe. He said the United Nations Organization was a United States tool, toadying to the capitalists in the United States-Cuba confrontation.

The effect of all this was to persuade those in United States positions of power to delay any decision concerning a Cuban adventure employing force, and instead to attempt a defence based upon all means *short* of force. The result was more vacillation and irresolution in the United States, and in Cuba a conviction born of astonishment that the most powerful nation in the world had a rotten core.

The Soviet Union funded and armed Castro's island, established KGB facilities in Cuba, created a masterfully organized subversion apparatus aimed at all Latin American nations, and did all it dared do to achieve an additional beachhead, preferably in Central or South America, on the mainland, and the United States which had a precedent based upon gunboat diplomacy for dealing with troublesome neighbours in the southern hemisphere, failed completely to devise counter-measures against the massive, very expert USSR campaign of infiltration and subversion.

Gunboats were anachronistic; the United States was no longer dealing with a small nation existing entirely within its own sphere. Cuba had become a Red satellite, a Soviet dependency. Nor was there or had there ever been anywhere in the Western Hemisphere, a counter-balancing organization genuinely comparable to the Soviet Union's KGB, and by 1960 it was too late to attempt the creation of one, even if the United States would have sanctioned such an idea, and that left only the option United States leaders liked least, and had been procrastinating about since Premier Khrushchev's threats and bombast: the use of force.

The considered alternative, in leadership circles, was worse: Soviet influence spreading throughout Latin America, and, inevitably, North America, the establishment of subversive networks throughout the hemisphere (which occurred regardless, in the 1960s), and an ultimate confrontation on a vast scale. Accordingly, it was reluctantly decided in early 1960 while Dwight D. Eisenhower was President to undertake a feasibility study, and the CIA was given this assignment. At this time Allen Dulles was director of the Central Intelligence Agency. His brother, John Foster Dulles, was President Eisenhower's Secretary of State.

Throughout the spring, summer and autumn of 1960 a number of plans were evolved, but none were submitted in a completed form to either President Eisenhower or the United States Joint Chiefs of Staff, whose approval would be required.

Not until January of 1961 did the CIA have what it considered a workable plan, and in the preceding November, during the presidential elections, John F. Kennedy emerged triumphant, President Eisenhower retired, and the only discussion of the Cuban situation which occurred between the retiring President Eisenhower, and the President-elect, Kennedy, occurred, according to Eisenhower, during their drive together to the inaugural ceremonies, when Eisenhower said he told Kennedy that the new leader and his administration would have to decide what was to be done.

Nevertheless, in implementation of its feasibility study the Central Intelligence Agency had already created training facilities for anti-Castro Cubans, euphemistically designated as 'freedom fighters', outside the United States, in Panama and Guatemala, and within the United States at Fort Meade, twenty miles from Washington, and in the backwater areas of Florida and Louisiana.

There was disapproval of the use of United States training facilities on the grounds that it would be impossible for the United States to deny participation in what was to be called strictly a Cuban affair, if the invaders had been trained in the United States, which was the epitome of naïvete in any event, since anti-Communists in Cuba's Escambray Mountains were being supplied by air-drops from United States aircraft, an operation which had been in progress for some time, and which was known by the Communists to be United States sponsored.

The situation when John F. Kennedy became president in 1961 was certainly not beyond recall, but neither had it been officially authorized except by the Central Intelligence Agency. Instructors at all bases including those in both Panama and Guatemala were from the United States armed forces. Equipment, armament, and funds came from United States sources. With initial preparations well under way, the original plan was submitted to President Kennedy in early 1961. It was later drastically revised, but as initially presented, it included a landing of invasion forces at the seaside town of Trinidad, a considerable distance from Havana on an estuary some three miles from the port city of Casilda on the Cuban south coast, and adjacent to the Escambray Mountains in an area hostile to the Communists. Aside from the navigable estuary, an adjacency to the sea and a population favourable to the overthrow of Castro's régime, there was also an airfield, plus excellent cover for ground operations.

Trinidad was the CIA's choice. It was later approved as the invasion site by the Joint Chiefs of Staff. The invasion force as initially envisaged, augmented and supported by the Central Intelligence Agency, consisted of an air squadron of sixteen World War II B-26 bombers, five C-46 and four C-54 unarmed transport aircraft, and no fighters even on a contingency basis.

It was common knowledge that Castro's air force of thirty aircraft included latest-model jet fighters. Since the CIA plan called for the destruction of Castro's air-arm on the ground, fighters were considered unnecessary.

The landing force, known as 'La Brigada 2506', consisted of 1,443 Cubans whose training left no room for improvement. They were highly proficient in every phase of invasion tactics, including marine landings, securing and administering subjected areas, and in paratroop drops. Mostly, they were Catholics, but there were also many Protestants, and some were Jews. A large number were blacks or had black forefathers.

To oppose Brigade 2506, Castro had armour, superior aircraft, and vastly greater numbers. He had the largest army in Latin America. But the CIA, as well as the Cubans, were knowledgeable in Latin American history, which is the story from Bolívar's time to the present of the triumph of numerically inferior zealots. In Cuba, for example, Fidel Castro began his 'war of liberation' with twelve men. Fulgencio Batista, Castro's predecessor, achieved power beginning with twenty-five men.

The morale of Brigade 2506 was very high. Defeat was inconceivable. With CIA backing, and anticipated United States armed support, no one doubted that Castro would be beaten. No general reliance was placed upon a popular uprising by CIA planners, even though the enthusiastic Cubans were certain this would obtain. The CIA plan was not based upon euphoric enthusiasm, but upon hard facts and sledgehammer tactics.

In this initial plan as submitted to President Kennedy the air-factor was paramount. It was the key and the crux of the entire affair (called Operation Pluto). It was also the only component of the invasion force which could achieve anything close to parity with the Communists.

In the original plan there were to be at least forty-eight air-strikes, by schedule, and more if required. These missions were to be flown against Cuba from the Central American mainland. (From Nicaragua, in fact, which had a strong anti-Communist government, and whose ruling family, the Somozas, had been CIA-affiliated for years.) The round-trip was a little short of fifteen hundred miles and given the fuel capacity of the invasion aircraft that allowed only thirty minutes over the target.

First, the free Cuban Air Force was to spearhead the invasion with *three* (not two, as subsequently reported) air attacks which were to destroy Castro's air force on the ground. On the assumption that the first two strikes would eliminate Castro's air-arm, the third sortie was to seek and destroy any Communist aircraft missed or subsequently made air-worthy, after the first two strikes, and it was also to give aerial cover when the ground forces approached the beaches.

The CIA was to replace lost or damaged aircraft. It was also to co-ordinate all Intelligence from within Cuba with the commanders of Brigade 2506. Finally, since supply as well as air-power was absolutely essential to success, the CIA had stockpiled at great expense the anticipated requirements for a successful invasion.

This was the CIA plan when John F. Kennedy became United States chief executive. Obviously, it could only succeed *as planned* providing its several parts were adequately co-ordinated, but especially its air-strike capability. Also, discreetly not mentioned in the event of disaster on the beach, it was tacitly understood among the United States military people entrusted with 'observation' that United States air and sea power would move in to succour and bring off the survivors.

In Cuban eyes there was a final indisputable factor which would ensure success : the United States, whether it acknowledged it or not, and through its Central Intelligence Agency, had organized, trained, supported, and was shortly now to transport, the invasion troops to their beachhead, as an ally of free Cubans. The success of their venture had been guaranteed by the most powerful nation in the world. Not a single free Cuban who embarked with the invasion force had a doubt that the United States was his friend and his ally.

The plan as submitted by the Central Intelligence Agency and approved by the Joint Chiefs of Staff, and implicitly believed in by the Cuban troops and their United States instructors, was in great measure the creation of a senior CIA official, Richard Bissell, an executive Clandestine Services officer, and, so it was rumoured, the probable successor to CIA Chief Allen Dulles, who was past retirement age (sixty-eight). As head of Clandestine Services since 1958, Richard Bissell had proved himself a highly competent, knowledgeable and capable Intelligence administrator. His original concept of the Cuban invasion was now to be studied by President Kennedy and his senior advisers, and what followed was a fair example of something history abounds in : very capable men in subordinate positions being used as scapegoats by very incapable men in higher positions.

President Kennedy's first error was in adhering to the premise that United States participation in the forthcoming invasion had to be kept secret. (Already, in early 1961, at least a dozen United States newspapers had printed stories, some with maps, about the proposed invasion, and the United States role in it.)

He instructed the Joint Chiefs of Staff to locate another landing-site, on the grounds that the popular resort-city of Trinidad was too well known and that world opinion would immediately assume there was United States involvement. He preferred some isolated site beyond the immediate reach of newsmen. In any event secrecy was to be paramount.

But in fact there was no secret. Nor had there been for many months. Even the Communist Cubans knew what impended. As early as the second week in January 1961, Raul Roa, Cuban Foreign Minister, had accused the United States of preparing and supporting an invasion force.

The Joint Chiefs of Staff made a reluctant reassessment and offered in place of the Trinidad-Casilda beachhead, an area known as Playa Girón, close by the Bay of Pigs. This decision was made in conjunction with an equally reluctant CIA.

Girón lay approximately a hundred miles farther down the Cuban coast than Trinidad, which put it even farther from Havana, where Castro's tanks and troops were concentrated, which, clearly, was in Girón's favour, as were two other factors; an airfield capable of accommodating bomber aircraft, and an almost total lack of Communist troops in the immediate vicinity.

There was an excellent reason for Castro's commanders to avoid keeping troops close by. Near Girón was the immense and unhealthy Cienaga de Zapata quagmire, a swamp reaching more than sixty miles in one direction, and twenty miles in another direction. It was a foetid place of disease, stench, alligators, malarial mosquitoes, and treacherous quicksand-like black mud.

It had three access roads and the revised Kennedy plan required parachute-dropped free Cubans to secure these routes as the other landings were being made by sea and air. Where the central road from Havana converged upon the area, bombers were to knock out Communist tank and mobile artillery columns when they appeared and destroy the road.

The major weakness of the Kennedy plan lay in the fact that

Lieutenant-General Vernon A. Walters, deputy director of the CIA from May 1972 and acting director from July to September 1973, and William E. Colby, director from September 1973

The Headquarters of the CIA in Langley, Virginia

Girón—or the Bay of Pigs—area, had no access to safety in the event of disaster. At Trinidad there were the nearby mountains. At Girón there was a deadly swamp, or the sea at the back of the invaders. Still, with aerial superiority assumed by the free Cubans and the CIA, although the Bay of Pigs was only reluctantly accepted as the new invasion site the chances of victory were still excellent. It was never the intention of the free Cubans, the Central Intelligence Agency, or the Joint Chiefs of Staff for the invasion force to remain at Girón longer than was mandatory to land men, armament and supplies. The invasion was to be vigorously pushed inland.

On 4th April 1961, President Kennedy presided over a State Department conference with Richard Bissell, Allen Dulles and General Charles Cabell of the Central Intelligence Agency, present, along with Kennedy aides, Richard Goodwin, Arthur Schlesinger Jr, McGeorge Bundy and Adolf Berle. Also in attendance were Douglas Dillon, Secretary of the Treasury, Dean Rusk, Secretary of State, and J. William Fulbright, Chairman of the Senate Foreign Relations Committee.

Representing the Joint Chiefs of Staff were General Lyman Lemnitzer, Chairman of the Joint Chiefs and Admiral Arleigh Burke, Chief of Naval Operations. There was also an Assistant Secretary of Defence, as well as an Assistant Secretary of State for Latin American Affairs, upon the periphery of this august conclave.

The revised (Kennedy) plan was reviewed and despite the earlier written as well as oral preferences for the Trinidad-Casilda area as given by the Joint Chiefs, Kennedy remained adamant. The invasion would take place at Girón. Richard Bissell was to supervise the operation. The invasion would occur Monday 17th April 1961.

There was one dissenter, Senator Fulbright called the undertaking immoral. Earlier he had called the Castro régime nothing more than a thorn in the flesh of the United States.

On Friday 14th April, free Cuban ground, sea, and air forces were alerted for action through a directive which said, among other things, that the free Cubans were 'to engage in amphibious and parachute landings, take, occupy, and defend beachheads in the area of Cochinos Bay and Playa Girón of the Zapata Swamps . . .'

Support and supply entailed the immediate delivery of over seventy tons of equipment, ammunition, arms, radios, etc., with an additional fifteen hundred tons to be sent in subsequently. The air squadron was made ready. In Havana, where the *Fidelistas* knew invasion was coming, the air waves vibrated with denunciations. And with fear. No one knew when, or where, the strikes would occur.

Between the 4th April State Department meeting and the eve of the actual invasion several of President Kennedy's aides and advisers including Arthur Schlesinger and Richard Goodwin who had zealously opposed the original CIA plan, worked just as zealously to undermine the Kennedy plan.

The result of this inter-administration factionalism was that although the President did not cancel the invasion, he became more and more concerned with secrecy, with methods which would minimize chances for discovery of the United States role. For example, he wanted the ships to beach the Brigade in the dark—this, in an area of razor-sharp coral reefs which were treacherous in broad daylight. He also wanted the aerial strikes held to an absolute minimum despite the fact that he had been clearly and repeatedly informed that the invasion's success was almost wholly dependent upon aerial support and supremacy.

He directed that these changes be made *without telling either the CIA or the Joint Chiefs of Staff*. By the time it became known that emasculation was in progress and despite the vigorous protests of the Joint Chiefs and the CIA senior executives involved, the men who were encouraging President Kennedy were in firm control at the White House level.

The first air attack, scheduled for dawn on 15th April and employing all free Cuba's sixteen bombers in order that complete success, which was so essential, would be assured, was changed by orders from President Kennedy. Only eight bombers were to participate and of the subsequent forty-eight missions to be flown the number was reduced to forty. One week before the date of invasion, again by Presidential order, the second air strike against Castro's air force and anti-aircraft installations was summarily cancelled altogether.

Again, by order of President Kennedy and at the instigation of his advisers the total number of flights, previously reduced from a minimum of forty-eight to forty, was now further reduced to a total of twenty-four flights.

Richard Bissell, his CIA superiors and the Joint Chiefs of Staff, discussed cancellation of the invasion, but ultimately decided against any such recommendation on the grounds that even as crippled as the project was, success remained possible providing President Kennedy did nothing further to hamstring it.

Three days before the first scheduled air attack against Castro's island was to occur, on 12th April, President Kennedy explained the United States position, when he told the press that not under any circumstances would there 'be an intervention in Cuba by United States armed forces', which clearly meant that the ally of free Cuba would not lift an arm or offer a hand in the event of disaster, but would remain neutrally offshore in ships and overhead in United States aircraft until the last free Cuban was killed or captured.

This Kennedy pronouncement was repeated at the United Nations, and was of course beamed to both Havana and Moscow, where, in both capitals, anxiety was high. In Moscow, because CIA Intelligence had turned up the fact that the Soviets, regardless of Premier Khrushchev's threats to bomb United States bases, were not adequately armed for a full confrontation with the United States, Kennedy's announcement amounted to one small hope. In Havana, where Castro had the largest army in Latin America (in 1961 one out of every thirty Cubans was in it), the Communists could finally anticipate fighting only one force, a numerically inferior one, better trained, armed, and motivated, perhaps, but now deprived of even the United States shadow.

The invasion began with the scheduled air strike at dawn on Saturday 15th April. The *Fidelistas* were caught looking in the wrong direction. Half of Castro's grounded aircraft were destroyed. Free Cuban losses were three bombers with only one hit by anti-aircraft fire resulting in casualties. The free Cubans were jubilant. The following day, Sunday 16th April, the free Cuban pilots were mustered for the briefing which was to precede the next strike, calculated to destroy Castro's remaining aircraft. The location of every remaining Castro aircraft was known as a result of both aerial reconnaissance and internal espionage.

Without explanation this final flight was cancelled. President Kennedy, again without notifying either the Joint Chiefs or the CIA, then *cancelled all further flights*, and with Brigade 2506 already on its way to Girón there were to be no bombers overhead to halt the mobile guns, tanks, and now also what remained of Castro's air power, which would shortly begin its triumphant sweep towards the Bay of Pigs.

As soon as Richard Bissell and the CIA's Deputy Director, General Charles Cabell, an Air Force officer with an impressive wartime record, were informed of President Kennedy's latest order, they immediately contacted Secretary of State Dean Rusk, and were informed that, now, political considerations had taken precedent over the advantages of ousting Cuba's Communists by force. In the face of the CIA's urgent pleas, as well as its dire predictions as to what must now follow at the Bay of Pigs, Secretary Rusk telephoned the President. Kennedy listened, then reiterated his stand : the aerial flights were cancelled, and United States forces offshore were not to intervene regardless of what occurred.

General Cabell personally telephoned the President. Kennedy was adamant. The first landing came ashore, was spectacularly successful, then Castro's air force swept in, his tanks were on the way, the invaders were overwhelmed by Cuban volunteers asking for guns, and what was certain triumphant slowly became a disaster.

In desperation, as reports reached Washington, the CIA pleaded with President Kennedy to rescind his orders prohibiting flights by the free Cuban Air Squadron. Admiral Burke, in exceptionally strong language, called on Kennedy to support the bogged-down, fiercely fighting free Cubans which the United States had put down at the Bay of Pigs. In the late afternoon of Wednesday 19th April, the free Cuban commander at Girón radioed to the United States ships offshore : 'I have nothing left to fight with. The enemy tanks are in position. Farewell . . .'

In three violent days the fighting was over. Castro had 1,199 survivors of Brigade 2506 as captives. The remainder were dead or missing.

Subsequently, President Kennedy blamed the disaster on the CIA. He forced the retirement of Director Allen Dulles, fired Richard Bissell, and forced out General Cabell, acts designed to encourage a belief that these men and the organization they were affiliated with were the real villains, and with a good politician's sure instinct for survival he successfully contrived so successfully to exploit the traditional silence of the intelligence community that even the free Cubans still believe his part in their betrayal was minimal, and the full blame belongs to the Central Intelligence Agency, which certainly has deserved criticism—many times—but, ironically, in this most famous illustration of its clandestine involvements, least deserved the blame for what happened at the Bay of Pigs.

7

Iran – an Example of Mixed Blessings

President Gerald Ford once said that the 'other side' does it and therefore the United States also does it, as though one inanity justifies an equal inanity, but his statement could have possessed a deeper meaning; he could have been implying that since the Soviet Union functions as a police state, the United States, in creating the western world's counter-foil to the Soviet KGB, could also become a police state, and while he probably did not mean that at all, the perils inherent in emulation *were* there. For example, the United States now has no less than eighteen Intelligence agencies, all flourishing, and all zealously compiling information on foes, friends, United States citizens, and even each other.

Like the KGB the United States over the years gradually increased the number of its CIA agents stationed in foreign embassies abroad until they outnumbered foreign service personnel, with the perhaps inevitable result that the boundary between implementing foreign policy and making it become blurred, and although it was a statement of Allen Dulles which called for a dissociation between the Intelligence function and the establishment of foreign policy, in fact it was during the Dulles era that this very dissociation was first abrogated, and the advice of British Intelligence experts that keeping policy and Intelligence operations under the same roof, or in the same family, would be a serious mistake, was ignored.

John Foster Dulles, President Eisenhower's Secretary of State, preferred Intelligence information supplied by his brother's skilled Intelligence organization to the reports of his own foreign service people, in the establishment of United States foreign policy, and, granting the probability that CIA information was certainly equal to, and possibly even more thorough than many embassy reports, the danger of Intelligence formulating policy was greater than the possible lack of depth in the embassy reports.

During the Dulles years there was no doubt that the Central Intelligence Agency *was* involved in the making of United States foreign policy. In the years following, with international turmoil increasing, and the United States role expanding in all areas where there was turmoil, the Dulles precedent continued strong, culminating finally, not in south-east Asia, as has been implied but in Cuba where the agency, seeking to function independently of the State Department, and on an equal footing with the War Department, became embroiled with the executive branch.

What occurred in Cuba was an example of mismanagement arising from a welter of conflicting—and often alienated—concepts. Left alone the Central Intelligence Agency probably would have broken Castro and his Communists in 1961 as it did Allende later in Chile, but hamstrung by the duplicity, the vacillation, and finally, by the stab-in-the-back techniques of a chief executive surrounded by erudite theorists, the result, aside from the deplorable disaster at Girón, was the first major power struggle between the Intelligence and executive branches of government for control of the policy-making procedures, since the agency's founding.

The executive branch won. At least on paper. President Kennedy, embarking upon a figurative tour of triumph informed all United States ambassadors that they, not the CIA's people, were the chief United States representatives abroad, and the man who succeeded John Foster Dulles as Secretary of State, Dean Rusk, once told a gathering of Foreign Service people that United States ambassadors were in charge of relations between the United States and the countries where they were positioned, and should 'if necessary . . . take charge of all officials who are . . . working with them', clearly meaning the CIA.

And yet, because the United States did not actually *have* a foreign policy, except the one formulated by the Dulles brothers which was founded upon containment of the Communist thrust through utilization of counter-active means which could best be carried out by counterfoil methods (subversion, harassment, etc.) through the CIA, in effect United States foreign, and ultimately even domestic policy, and the United States Intelligence effort, were one and the same.

This specific lack of an alternative option made the CIA and the KGB more than ever similar and there were any number of instances where international reaction to both organizations was the same.

Also, the 'blessings' derived were quite often identical. The KGB master-minded a dozen *coups* around the world, poured money, armament and technical aid into dozens of countries, most of whom accepted every contribution, then threw out its ingratiating benefactors. What Egypt, recipient of hundreds of millions of dollars' worth of Soviet aid, did to the Soviets, Indonesia did to the United States.

The degeneration of United States policy into a 'monkey-see, monkey-do' emulation of KGB and Supreme Soviet political as well as Intelligence functions could scarcely *not* have encouraged worldwide hostility since the United States role had become so little different, in most minds, from the Soviet role. Even United States successes, as in Iran where the Intelligence role was indistinguishable from the foreign policy role, amounted to a very uncomfortable mixed blessing, and became an excellent example of how 'saving' a country's sovereignty could damned near bankrupt the 'saviour', while at the same time suggesting to discerning policy-makers that not *all* the crosses were to be found on Calvary, when a powerful nation, lacking *real* alternatives to Communist oppression, substituted a variety of domination different in direction, but otherwise identical in purpose to the purpose of an enemy, and succeeded.

Another factor to be considered was the equation of time. Democratic administrations came and went, subject to the whims of electorates, but historic traditions, social pyramids and natural environments remained largely unalterable in the face of temporary political expediencies. What occurred in Iran in 1953 created political ripples which widened, and continued to widen for twenty years, without actually changing the basic Iranian ethos very much, although they had quite dramatic and unsettling repercussions elsewhere. Time was the determining factor, and in Iran time was not on the side of those whose preoccupation was with conditions which, while existent in 1953, were anything but existent in 1973. The result was that time created a vortex which sucked the United States into a whirlpool it has to this day been unable to extricate itself from, although in twenty years the United States had sufficient time to evolve *some* kind of political and social philosophy which could have superseded, and been better than the Dulles brothers' strategy of containment.

Everything, it seemed, was susceptible to change except United States foreign policy. It was locked in time.

When the CIA offered suggestions about Iran based upon analyses from the Intelligence sector neither the executive nor administrative branches of government assumed the initiative beyond encouraging the CIA to act in a representative capacity, and what followed was best epitomized by the axiom that *any* action was better than *no* action.

The flaw to this was simply that what ensued in Iran from 1953 onward was powerful CIA support for Shah Mohammed Reza Pahlevi, a man of monumental avarice and conceit, and after twenty years of coddling, the compliant kitten became a very large egocentric tiger.

The role of the CIA was to support stability in Iran. It succeeded. The role of United States leaders was to create protective hedges, and they also succeeded, for a time, but by 1973 they had failed. Reza Pahlevi became the worst threat to the industrialized West since the Great Depression, and remains so to this day.

His country, which contains 636,293 square miles and a population of 32,000,000, has a largely arid terrain. Until very recently less than a quarter of Iran's agricultural land was irrigated, and while dazzling splendour existed at the top, crushing poverty and squalor existed elsewhere.

The country possesses a variety of valuable mineral deposits but its main wealth lies in its oil, where development currently under way may very well exceed estimates. Thirty per cent of the population is illiterate, and factionalism has historically blighted most efforts to ensure harmony. Iranians, for centuries known as Persians, have enjoyed the blessings of miscegenation for generations; they are a mixture of Arabs, Turks, Afghans and Mongols.

Currently Iran is colourful, ancient, and proud, but politically it has been a backwater—although a strategically valuable one—susceptible to the influence of its neighbours, archaic in sentiment, and until quite recently, unpredictable in its politics.

To the Russians of earlier times the Iranian plateau was a temptation for expansion towards a warm-water seacoast, but only under the accelerated ambition of the Soviets was this desire to reach the Indian Ocean by way of Iran's adjacency to the Persian Gulf actively pursued by peaceful means. However, while Soviet force could certainly have overrun Iran, there was another, and for the Soviets, a very real danger. Iran was a valued source of petroleum to the powerful Western industrial nations. It could not be expected that the West would view the loss of an oil supply stoically.

But there *was* a way. The Soviet Union encouraged a tough old Iranian, Mohammed Mossadegh, a visionary leftist with the instincts of a hungry fox, to make a bid for power, which he did in 1951 during the course of a carefully contrived near-uprising in Iran, and to prevent internal trouble the boyish Shah, Mohammed Pahlevi, was forced to appoint Mossadegh Premier.

At once Soviet 'technicians' arrived in the country, the unpopular Iranian Communist Party (the *Tudeh*) was encouraged, and Premier Mossadegh, a wily politician, utilized the ploy of most native leaders seeking all popular support. He defied the old colonial powers, but particularly Great Britain which controlled the Anglo-Iranian Oil Company, by moving to nationalize foreign holdings in his country.

In this he was encouraged by the Soviets. The Anglo-Iranian Oil Company had been practically supporting Iran since about the time of the First World War through oil royalties. The Soviets, who had traditionally accomplished their designs best in political and economic vacuums, guided Mossadegh into a genuine catastrophe, for while Iranian nationalism might support the Premier, neither it nor he could survive if Iran descended into bankruptcy, and ultimately, actual chaos. But the Soviets could survive such a calamity quite well.

The result of nationalization and expropriation was swift retaliation by the industrial nations, including the United States. Iranian oil was put under boycott. But in the United States that was only the beginning for although CIA Director Allen Dulles was to say later that Mohammed Mossadegh had not demonstrated leftism, there were others, including British Intelligence which knew better, and as the oil boycott began to have an effect in Iran and the country's already frail and ailing economy was deprived of its best source of nourishment, Mossadegh, virtual dictator of Iran by 1952, turned to the Soviet Union in open acknowledgement of his debt to the Kremlin, and also for succour. At this juncture the CIA began an active campaign in Iran. It had a worthwhile *entrée* through a former chief of the New Jersey State Police, H. Norman Schwartzkopf who had established not only Iran's modern police establishment, but also ran Iran's Intelligence organization. Schwartzkopf was a personal friend of Shah Mohammed Pahlevi. He was also anathema to Mossadegh, the Soviet 'technicians', and of course the flourishing *Tudeh*.

There were other Americans in Iran, besides CIA agents, who arrived as the country's economic plight worsened, for while Central Intelligence Agents, and their 'in place' spies, infiltrated the *Tudeh*, the Iranian armed forces, and the national bureaucracy, the real need was for some variety of prompt economic assistance. If order collapsed, all the CIA agents together could not prevent the Soviets from crossing the common border to 'ensure the safety of its nationals and restore order'. The United States State Department allocated stop-gap funds in the order of $1,600,000 for immediate use by the Iranian government in 1951, and the following year made an additional grant of $23,000,000.

That was only the beginning of a financial tidal wave which, as the contest for control of Iran quickened, saw, by the year 1965, the United States pour $857,000,000 into the country, and also saw the USSR send in another $330,000,000.

But, once some degree of stability was achieved the real secret struggle began. Mossadegh, who actually possessed an admirable toughness while never appearing to be tough at all—he frequently broke into tears, even in public—conspired with Soviet Intelligence agents to achieve a double *coup*. Once it was discovered that the United States, despite its approval of the oil boycott, would pour astonishing amounts of money into Iran to maintain what seemed to be a friendly government, Premier Mossadegh conspired to ally his country with the Soviet Union, and simultaneously call upon the United States to send more money. Patently, there would eventually be a *dénouement*, but by that time the Premier hoped to have been able thoroughly to fleece the United States.

United States aid continued to arrive, Iran's foreign exchange difficulties were at last alleviated, and Mohammed Mossadegh's avarice increased. In May of 1953 he demanded that the United States increase its aid to Iran, the alternative to immediate compliance being that Mossadegh would bind his nation to the

Soviet Union through treaties of mutual defence and economic assistance.

The threat of an Iran-USSR economic pact was not as alarming to the United States leadership as the threat of a mutual defence pact, which would put Soviet arms not only in Iran, but in the Persian Gulf.

While this overt situation existed the CIA's covert campaign was also progressing. Every attempt by Mossadegh and the Communists to discredit the Shah was countered. The CIA's best hope lay in the possibility of Mohammed Pahlevi, a likeable, energetic, popular ruler, retaining his throne. The Communist Intelligence agents did all in their power to belittle His Majesty, while CIA agents, and funds, did all in their power to sustain the Shah's popularity.

The crux was the Shah himself. With his popularity being ensured by CIA manoeuvres, and while Premier Mossadegh and his Soviet Intelligence advisers conspired to overthrow him, Mohammed Pahlevi was compelled to show himself as the courageous man of prescience and capability his people thought he was, and that the CIA was working tirelessly to compel him to be.

Finally, the United States replied to Mossadegh's demands with an unequivocal refusal to be blackmailed. At the same time Allen Dulles took a vacation in Europe, flying to his World War II home, Switzerland.

Premier Mossadegh reacted to the United States refusal with ire, and at the same time the CIA administrator in charge of the Iranian affair, Kermit Roosevelt, thought it was now time for the Shah to take a stand in opposition to his leftist Premier. His Majesty, assured of adequate United States support, was uneasy about a direct confrontation despite CIA assurances. United States Ambassador Loy Henderson, after a meeting with His Majesty, also went on vacation—to Switzerland. At the same time His Majesty's very capable sister, Princess Ashraf, had an audience with His Majesty, after which she too flew to Switzerland.

Three days after Dulles arrived in Switzerland, on 13th August 1953, the Shah, having conferred with his old associate H. Norman Schwartzkopf, announced that Mossadegh was no longer Premier, and appointed in his place Major-General Fazlollah Zahedi, a national police and Intelligence commander—and also a close associate and personal friend of H. Norman Schwartzkopf.

In Switzerland, Allen Dulles had reports from Ambassador Henderson and Princess Ashraf to ponder, while in Iran Premier Mossadegh summoned Iranian troops to his residence, and when the Shah's emissary arrived with the official notification of his ouster, Mossadegh had the messenger, a colonel of the Shah's palace guard, imprisoned, and immediately denounced both his ouster and Shah Mohammed Pahlevi.

The CIA had been prepared for this contingency, and to ensure that their best hope for ultimate triumph would not be either imprisoned as the colonel of the palace guard had been, or, worse yet, assassinated, they immediately had His Majesty and his queen flown to safety in Rome, which was conveniently available to Switzerland. Then, with the aid of the Shah's friend, General Schwartzkopf, the CIA undertook a very extensive and very thorough campaign of bribery.

It cost the United States approximately $10,000,000 to buy back Mossadegh's chief supporters to the side of the Shah, and it was accomplished in something less than a week. United States dollars literally rained down upon Iran, the little destitute, largely illiterate oil emirate whose survival for decades had been a hand-to-mouth affair. During those fateful few days army commanders appeared in Teheran with their troops, bureaucrats, government leaders, and even the Soviet 'technicians', existed in an un-real atmosphere of complete uncertainty. No one in that part of the world had ever before actually seen a CIA campaign mounted. Rumours were everywhere, no one knew exactly what was going to happen, but as those millions of dollars were dispersed, it gradually became clear that Mohammed Mossadegh was being drowned by them, and since no one cared to be associated with a losing party, support for His Majesty increased considerably.

The CIA, utilizing Communism's oldest tactic of creating a vacuum, then exploiting it, now organized a typical Iranian street demonstration, a colourful parade of dancers, singers, jugglers, even costumed contortionists—all strictly coached, armed and ready.

Iranians crowded forth to watch as the noisy convocation proceeded through the capital. Many of the onlookers were guards from Premier Mossadegh's residential compound. Other troops, led by officers who opposed Mossadegh and had remained loyal to Shah Mohammed Pahlevi, were also in the capital, but were kept away from the noisy celebration at the ready.

When the procession had achieved its purpose, which was to put onlookers in a sympathetic, mob-oriented frame of mind, the jugglers, dancers and singers suddenly erupted into a roaring horde of activists shouting their support of the Shah, and their denunciation of Premier Mossadegh. Simultaneously, loyal army commanders ordered the attack upon Mossadegh's troops. Crowds ran howling through the streets in support of His Majesty. Mossadegh's partisan soldiers, largely disorganized, fought back, but with very little hope, because CIA military tactics, equal to their dollar-inundation tactics, were overwhelmingly superior.

By midnight, 14th August 1953, Mossadegh's troops, outnumbered, and outmanoeuvred, were compelled to surrender with their backs to the outer walls of the Premier's official residence. Inside, the Premier, attired in gaudy silk pyjamas rolled upon his bed weeping. He was taken into custody, word was sent to Switzerland that Shah Mohammed Pahlevi's forces had triumphed, and His Majesty returned, confirmed General Zahedi as Premier, some of the Soviet Intelligence agents packed their bags, and it was announced that through a 'popular' uprising the Iranian people had restored their country's sacred sovereignty. No one said a word about Norman Schwartzkopf, Kermit Roosevelt, or the CIA.

Iran, 'saved' for the West with its thirteen per cent of known oil deposits (in 1953), became henceforth a ward of the United States State Department, and although the CIA remained strong in Iran, and to this day maintains a very large apparatus in the country, it was the State Department which—finally—inaugurated a United States foreign policy programme. An international board of directors assumed control of Iranian oil production and distribution, which ultimately achieved a $300,000,000 revenue for the country.

Pro-Western governments, satisfactory to the United States State Department, came and went, every one of them corrupt, and despite its entirely adequate oil income, conditions became so bad that the United States, aside from outright grants running into the millions of dollars, had to subsidize the country with a regular infusion of money at the rate of five million dollars monthly, most of which was stolen, sent to numbered bank accounts in Switzerland, and totally squandered.

Shah Mohammed Pahlevi's Intelligence chief, General Haj Ali Kia, had a budget of $1,500,000 monthly for his espionage agency, which, by most Western Intelligence standards was not exorbitant, except that General Kia was the sole member of his 'bureau'.

By 1961 the Shah's latest pro-Western Premier reported that Iran's national debt stood at $500,000,000, and that the nation verged on insolvency and bankruptcy. The State Department, which had condoned every government subsequent to the overthrow of Mohammed Mossadegh, and which had not insisted on accurate or adequate accountings for the millions wasted, or the millions stolen, adhered to its same policy: if a government was pro-Western, it was an ally. But Iran, where millions of destitute peasants witnessed the splendour at the top and continued to exist in squalor at the bottom, became easy prey for the now-flourishing Communist party. In 1961, old Mohammed Mossadegh re-surfaced from prolonged house-confinement and enormous throngs converged to shout for his return to power. He was returned to confinement and nothing changed; the United States still pumped money into Iran faster than the oil consortium could pump petroleum out, until, finally, the Shah, in consort with other oil-producing nations, encouraged nationalization. Then, also in consort with the other oil producers, his government embarked on a pricing-spiral, an oil boycott of Western nations, and another spiralling increase in oil prices until the wealth of the industrial nations was being drained away into Arab treasuries faster than the West could generate capital—and still nothing changed in Iran for the majority of people, until the year 1974, when His Majesty finally embarked upon a number of public works programmes which could very well buy him the support by 1975 the CIA bought for him in 1953.

Nevertheless, this product of the United States State Department ruthlessly suppresses opposition through one of the finest espionage networks extant. The number of secret police (SAVAK) personnel is roughly three times the size of the CIA (in 1974). It has spies worldwide, secret prisons where an estimated 25,000 dissidents are confined, and employs an informer corps estimated to include one out of every ten Iranians. Secret executions are reputed to be commonplace, and while Teheran, the Iranian capital, still lacks an adequate sewage system and the majority of Iranians still exist on a sub-standard level, His Majesty has embarked upon a programme to make Iran the strongest nation in the Arab world, and one of the strongest and most financially influential nations in the entire world. In 1973 he spent four billion dollars for the latest weapons in the United States arsenal, on the financial side he bought strong support in Bangladesh by giving $100,000,000 in grants, he loaned over a billion dollars to British industrialists, entered into joint economic ventures with the Italians to the extent of three billion dollars, moved into Africa with $10,000,000 for Senegal, bought a quarter interest in Germany's Krupp *Konzern* for over $100,000,000 while in the United States he bought friends at the Grumman Aircraft Corporation by investing $75,000,000 in that company, and purchased influence with the United States-based World Bank by depositing one billion dollars with that institution.

While the paradoxical Shah spreads largesse, and actually does much good, Iran is a police state, and the current CIA position in his country is stronger than it was back in 1953. Present United States ambassador to Iran is the former Director of the CIA, Richard M. Helms, the first chief executive of United States Intelligence ever appointed to ambassadorial rank.

Mohammed Pahlevi spearheaded the OPEC's (oil producing and exporting countries) 400 per cent increase in oil prices, which created a crisis among the industrial nations. Yet he remains pro-Western. At the same time he is friendly with the Soviets, scolds the United States, as when he said, '. . . we will not be dictated to' in response to United States admonitions over the oil pricing spiral, and furthers a private personality cult by decreeing that Iranian newspapers report favourably on the royal family at least once a week.

But Mohammed Pahlevi, although sustained in office by the CIA, remains a product of the US State Department, not the CIA. It was in accordance with the State Department's expressed policy that the CIA functioned in Iran, and still functions in Iran.

The State Department considers His Majesty its foremost ally on the Persian Gulf. For that reason there is small likelihood that any relief for the oil-consuming industrialized West will originate in Iran, or be suggested to Iran's monarch by Washington.

8

Towards the Maelstrom

Currently, and in the immediate past, the Intelligence view of the world has been a result of the geographic location, the security and defence aspects, and the vital interests of ideologies—not nations.

At one time the Intelligence view was exclusively national. For example, Britain, for more than four hundred years spied zealously in order to protect its particular vital interests. So did France and Germany. So did Poland, Hungary, and so did all the world states whose survival depended upon preventing a particular nation or alliance from acquiring political, economic or military supremacy. When Germany consisted of a dozen petty principalities, each with its own laws, customs, and insignificant prince, espionage and counter-espionage had influence in every area between the Baltic Sea and the Adriatic Sea, greater than that of all the ever-marching hosts. Then consolidation and interdependence narrowed the scope of Intelligence while at the same time they widened the boundaries of nations, and gradually, again as in Germany, the ideology of Prussia ultimately became the ideology of Austria, suggesting that nationalism was yielding to ideology, and when this occurred (it is still occurring), while some states retained their nationalism other states surrendered their individuality and became satellites of larger ideological systems, with a result that many historic viewpoints in such areas as politics, international relations, and Intelligence, were completely changed.

After all the centuries of fierce, costly wars of defence all the intrigues, and all the undisputed convictions that every nation and every individual was absolutely entitled to defend freedom, this ancient, honoured and historic concept just simply died of old age. Poland, for example, whose bone-pile of slain patriots would dwarf mountains, whose dedication to freedom was fierce and total for generations, quite abruptly yielded freedom with scarcely a second thought, and this most motivating of all Polish convictions for so long was replaced by a variety of subservience which usually only arises as a result of slavery, behind which the craving remains, except that in Poland even that vestige lacked a heartbeat.

In the 1950s Polish Intelligence discovered CIA agents working out of a West German headquarters, within Poland's borders. Those who made this discovery were *Polish* Intelligence people, not Soviet personnel. The purpose of the infiltrators was to fund, arm, and organize, Polish resistance. They were uncovered, apprehended, and imprisoned. The national, independent view, was dead. It had become sublimated, or replaced by, the ideological view. In Poland, native authorities were subservient to the idea that what benefited their Soviet overlords, benefited Poland. What had been a sovereignty had become a satrapy. Ideology, not nationalism, mattered.

Poland was no rare example and neither was the Soviet philosophy the only ideology, but as the political boundaries widened and the economic interdependencies became more operational, nationalism faded, ideology replaced it, and there was no way for sovereign states to avoid being pulled into one ideological vortex or the other, and even the remaining free states were fully tainted. Canada, Japan, Indonesia, Sweden, Portugal, Spain, Mexico, Norway, Cambodia, even anciently neutral Switzerland, every free state from Britain to Iceland, was tainted. Nationalism, may it rest in peace, was dead. There were only two super-forces in the world; every action of every country on earth was taken in response to an attitude of a super-power. Every defence posture which in former times had rested firmly upon individual nationality, now rested upon an alliance with one super-power or the other. All politics, economics, pacts and treaties, all philosophies, aspirations, and even food consumption, were dependent upon a nation's status, favoured or not, with a super-power. Everyone became a member of one camp or the other, and voluntary willingness had nothing to do with it. Nationalism had died quietly some time between 1945 and 1950. Before 1945 small nations could still influence world events. After 1950 only one of two super-powers could do that, and when there remains only one super-power, then will begin the long day's march into night. But before that cataclysm occurs, *if* it occurs, the primary factor on both sides which will increasingly proliferate will be the Intelligence factor, and although it is very easy to decry and disparage *all* Intelligence, this has to be the shortsighted view, because nothing prevents an aggressor from aggression as well as a fear that he may be unable satisfactorily to prevail, and his best source of this information is not negotiation or diplomacy, it is espionage.

For the West, a Central Intelligence Agency which acquires more blame than it deserves, produces more blunders than it should, and accomplishes successes which are not properly nor adequately implemented by a United States State Department with an incredible history of foreign policy failures, may not be the best *answer*, but thus far it has been the best *alternative*.

Perhaps someone should apologize for the CIA's failures and for its blunders, because inevitably these are swiftly picked up and exploited, especially by an unfriendly news media which can rhetorically denounce anything it cares to, but there have been successes too, although, as in Guatemala, Chile, and Iran, their subsequent mixed blessings have produced some over-sized headaches, which were less a result of the CIA's participation than a result of the State Department's absolute and chronic ineptness, therefore, if apologies are required, State should inaugurate the procedure. It would be as reasonable to blame an attorney who has successfully prosecuted a murderer, for what the murderer does when he is released from prison, as it would be to blame the CIA for the wholesale failures of United States Foreign Policy, which simply has never offered a truly beneficial alternative to oligarchic oppression, and which therefore, once the CIA has moved out, as in Chile, reinstates and reinforces the same bad system which led to trouble in the first place.

On the other hand, the CIA's initial successes, which were accomplished more with money than Intelligence expertise, fostered a costly precedent which became a CIA crutch; the free use of vast sums of money rather than political manipulation. Nowhere was this demonstrated better than, first in Iran, and secondly in south-east Asia. In the latter area, because the involvement was vastly greater the example was better. Nevertheless, and without any intention at all of excusing or condoning what was done, it has long been a fact of political life that bribery by whatever name one chooses to call it—a 'grant' a 'gift', or just plain wages for mercenaries—as a means for successful corruption is anything but a CIA innovation. Further, in fairness, and although the cost was ruinous as well as appalling, the CIA at least *had* the funds to use, during its early years, while it was acquiring the kind of practical experience it needed to operate with any hope of success against a vastly larger, better-funded, and more entrenched Soviet Intelligence system.

Intelligence work can no longer be accomplished inexpensively, any more than fielding an army can. The day when a Union soldier in a cheap wicker basket attached to a bag of gas and secured to a tree on the ground by a length of rope, could soar into the air and spy out the Confederate lines, passed into history over a hundred years ago. As the era of narrow national boundaries, with their accompanying little resplendent armies wearing white gaiters and powdered wigs, yielded to larger hegemonies and less colourful and more expensive armies, Intelligence-gathering also became correspondingly more costly. Along with all the practical experience acquired by the CIA in the rather busy year of 1954, the costs kept increasing. The overthrow of Arbenz Guzman in Guatemala during the spring and summer, followed by the sophisticated Berlin tunnel in the summer and autumn, were expensive successes, and as the years passed and multi-million-dollar spy-in-the-sky satellites to a great degree replaced cloak-and-dagger procedures, Intelligence-gathering costs soared unbelievably, but the curse was not actually the cost, it was the confounded *necessity* for espionage.

Bribery, too, kept pace with more acceptable varieties of international inflation, but there were many instances of flagrant waste. Nevertheless, agency sophistication increased and despite what ultimately became an exorbitantly expensive operation, it was largely the improving capabilities of the CIA which hastened the arrival of East-West *détente.* For twenty years Soviet Intelligence techniques had replaced old-time armed procedures, moving initially into contrived vacuums, with success. Operational CIA opposition, in all the places cited up to now in former chapters, increasingly successful as the 1950s yielded to the '60s, ultimately compelled a re-assessment by the Soviets, and the critics who came later, in the '70s, to maintain that CIA involvement was immoral, were either deliberately or ignorantly unaware that a secret war involving millions of people and billions of dollars, the future security of the West, and their own freedom and safety—not to mention their standard of living—was being fought.

Direction of the agency through these years was largely the responsibility of one man, Allen Welsh Dulles. In fact Allen Dulles served the CIA longer than any director to date. He was Deputy Director from 9th February 1953 to 26th February 1953—two weeks—and Director from 26th February 1953, until his 'retirement', 29th November 1961, subsequent to the Bay of Pigs *débâcle*, a period of nine years. His tenure and his Intelligence philosophy left their impression, indubitably, but while techniques changed vastly—from covert espionage to satellite-scanning photographic over-flights—the Dulles basics remained fundamental CIA policies.

The man who succeeded Allen Dulles, John Alex McCone, Director from 29th November 1961 until 28th April 1965, CIA chief during the Kennedy years, came into Intelligence work with doubts and misgivings about the CIA's capabilities. He was the individual who arranged for ITT co-operation with the CIA in the plot to overthrow Chile's Marxist chief of state Salvador Allende in 1973, and as though in confirmation of the Soviet allegation that the CIA served only the exploiting capitalist interests, McCone was a member of the Board of Directors of International Telephone and Telegraph.

What McCone learned about CIA capabilities achieved its greatest impetus when United States Intelligence revealed the fact, in the summer of 1962, that Soviet ballistic missiles had been installed in Communist Cuba, proving what a little prescience in 1961 could have done despite the contrary opinions of such people as Senator Fulbright and Arthur Schlesinger: that Red Cuba *was* a threat to the nations of the western hemisphere, and although it was subsequently claimed the missile discovery was a result of high-altitude spy-plane over-flights, in fact the initial reports came to the Central Intelligence Agency from 'in place' spies in Cuba.

McCone—and millions of others, especially in the United States—agonized through the subsequent US-USSR confrontation which preceded an alleged withdrawal of the missiles (in exchange for the United States concessions which to this day have not been fully revealed).

By the time Alex McCone was replaced as CIA Director by Vice Admiral William F. Raborn (USN-R), who served from 28th April 1965 until 30th June 1966—fourteen months—he had learned that CIA capability was adequate for successes, and failures, exactly as with any other large federal agency, with the distinction being that, with the CIA, because of the nature of its involvements its successes could not be either officially announced, or very often 'sanitized' to look entirely virtuous, while its failures arrived with the morning coffee—or tea—in every newspaper in the world.

It was the three ensuing directors who became victims of an ethos created largely through CIA intervention in the Soviet-KGB scheme of infiltration and subversion; the environment of Soviet penetration and conquest which was upset by CIA oppositions, forcing a change in Soviet policy and KGB procedures in the 1960s.

Richard Helms became CIA Director on 30th June 1966 and served in that capacity until 2nd February 1973, a period of seven years. As the current United States Ambassador to Iran, Helms remains high in United States Intelligence officialdom, although no longer publicly connected with the Central Intelligence Agency.

Helms' successor, and another former agency chief who was moved into a critical post which was Intelligence-oriented, was James R. Schlesinger, who served as CIA Director from 2nd February 1973, until 2nd July 1973—five months—and subsequently became United States Secretary of Defence.

These men, McCone, Raborn, and Schlesinger, along with one other, current Agency Director, William E. Colby, who became CIA chief on 4th September 1973, (between Schlesinger's departure in July 1973 and Colby's appointment in September 1973, an Assistant Director, General Vernon A. Walters, held temporary office as Director) were the agency's chief executives during the crucial period of change, and three of them, McCone, Schlesinger, and Colby, became the targets of the accusations, vilification and denunciation which were a powerfully integral part of that change.

The CIA involvement in Vietnam, throughout all south-east Asia in fact, beginning with the support of ill-fated (Jean Baptiste) Ngo Dinh Diem in 1960, and which was largely influenced by a CIA Clandestine Services officer of considerable talent and force,

Colonel (later General) Edward Lansdale, and which became the agency's worst involvement, one which it still has been unable to extricate itself from, arrived on the heels of a simultaneous involvement in the Congo, and another one in Tibet, the last two practically unknown outside the agency, but the first, Vietnam, badly damaged the agency's image, as that conflict dragged on and on, exhausting American patience and bringing down upon the heads of all United States officialdom committed to the support of South Vietnam, the anger of United States taxpayers, as well as the indignation of many people, worldwide.

It was this spirit of disapproval during the later Vietnam war years, which seemed to presage the era of change, not only among United States citizens but in general throughout the world, and while there was no doubt but that much of this disapprobation was Soviet-inspired, the fact remained that an era of change *had* arrived, although the agency continued to function in its traditional manner. It was involved in a clandestine effort in Tibet secretly to arm and organize followers of the Dalai Lama against the Chinese Communists who had, some years earlier, successfully invaded Tibet and replaced the Dalai Lama with their own Panchen Lama. The operation was a failure; it could not have succeeded in any case. A few thousand Tibetan horsemen could hardly have prevailed in any serious attempt to oust the Chinese, whose border with Tibet has, since ancient times, sheltered Chinese armies capable of overrunning Tibet at any time.

In the Congo, at roughly the same time, the CIA moved to the support of the Mobutu government, threatened by Communist-funded and indoctrinated dissidents, and although the initial CIA programme was based upon bribery, which proved very effective, the dissidents turned to violence and the United States government Intelligence-control-agency, and the President, authorized CIA participation in an active role, the government's position being, as always, to maintain in power a pro-Western ally.

The agency dispatched experienced United States military advisers who at once created an effective paramilitary force, including an 'air force' of B-26 bombers owned by the CIA. (These planes were probably a residue from the Bay of Pigs, which misadventure had occurred three years earlier; it was subsequently discovered that, in fact, some of those B-26s were piloted by free Cubans.)

By the standards of most CIA joint ventures the Congo affair was relatively inexpensive. Some cost was advanced by Belgian and other industrialists with investments in the Congo, and while this would inevitably lead to allegations—as it would almost ten years later in Chile—that the agency was an instrument of capitalism, the agency, and in this case the United States government, was far less concerned with foreign-controlled industry in the Congo than it was in crushing a subversion attempt and maintaining a pro-Western government in power, which was done when Joseph Mobutu, with CIA funds, advisers and arms, and also by his own regional popularity, achieved supremacy over several unbelievably capricious opponents including Patrice Lumumba, and also over a poorly organized Communist commitment.

There was, then, a failure in Tibet and a success in the Congo. Several years earlier there had been a success in Guatemala, and, later, a failure in the 1958 CIA-supported Indonesian uprising whose purpose had been to oust President Sukarno. These episodes and others like them occupied the agency as international conditions appeared to be subtly altering. For one thing, the Soviet effort began to harden as KGB efforts were either thwarted, as in Guatemala and the Congo, or were imperilled by United States threats, as in south-east Asia.

Another hint of change appeared worldwide when political leaders and news analysts began to suggest that in this vast and growing war between hostile Intelligence monoliths, regardless of who triumphed, hundreds of thousands of people and entire nations were being systematically destroyed.

This change was discernible as the United States and the Soviet Union manoeuvred into position for what was to become the CIA's greatest involvement, and although the Intelligence presence which had historically preceded armies, was established in the area of contention—south-east Asia—first, its function was paramilitary. The accumulation of Intelligence throughout the Vietnam War was less to inform Washington than it was to promote co-operation and success for armed forces in service against the aggressor DRVN, (Democratic Republic of North Vietnam) including the forthcoming United States armed services, the ARVN, (Army of South Vietnam) and the clandestine armed forces recruited, armed and funded by the Central Intelligence Agency.

However, the Intelligence role was to become more totally encompassing than the role of the United States armed forces, for while a hypocritical morality was to deny US armed forces open access to adjacent sovereignties, the CIA clandestine operations spilled over into Laos, Cambodia and Thailand, where the Communist effort was also active.

In this area the Communist attitude was to promote its most formidable opposition, and was to achieve its most violent apex, and out of this rawest of brutal confrontations was ultimately to arise the most outspoken worldwide denunciation, even though many of the loudest and most vehement denunciators did not actually understand that what was in progress was as much a war between Intelligence monoliths as it was a gory ideological confrontation.

In this south-east Asian conflict the CIA's Special Operations Division was to expand greatly. It was, at this time, under the same Richard Helms who later became CIA Director, and who replaced Richard Bissell whose credibility had declined sharply after the Bay of Pigs disaster. *All* phases of the United States Intelligence function increased during the Indo-China War, as did every operational military aspect of the United States, and when it was later stated or implied, as was done in the Marks-Marchetti book *The CIA and the Cult of Intelligence*, that agency involvement was excessive, the questions arose: excessive in comparison to what? Certainly not in comparison to the US military presence, which numbered into the millions. In comparison, then, to the enemy Intelligence apparatus? Hardly; the Democratic Republic of North Vietnam (DRVN) Intelligence apparatus, operating as a segment of the Indo-Chinese Communist Party (ICP), which had been actively in existence since the 1930s with networks throughout all the former French possessions including Cambodia and Laos, derived Intelligence information from one of the largest espionage systems in the world, with information being fed to Hanoi from every level of village, governmental, and even military, life, from throughout all Indo-China—or south-east Asia as it was called by 1960.

As a result of this vast and efficient espionage operation functioning in supposedly neutral Laos, the DRVN leadership conceived a sound strategy of infiltrating a vast armed force into Laos to strike westerly across the Laotian-South Vietnam border, attacking both the South Vietnamese and their allies, the Americans, Australians, and others, from the rear, the objective being to drive them towards the South China Sea, and as though to implement this idea, in 1962 at Geneva an agreement was reached whereby foreign armed forces were prohibited from operating in Laos, although DRVN troops and their local partisans were already there, with more coming.

The consequence of this prohibition, held to be binding upon the United States, was that President John F. Kennedy authorized the Central Intelligence Agency to increase its covert Laotian presence, not entirely as an Intelligence organization, but also as a paramilitary establishment whose purpose was to prevent a DRVN attack from the West.

The consequences were, unhappily for little Laos, chaotic, for every effort to sustain a pro-Western Laotian government and prevent the attack from the West, resulted in equal parts of success and failure, while at the same time an infusion of United States funds to the extent of $300,000,000 annually, hopelessly ruined the simple, and traditional Laotian way of life, a fact the uncommitted world-regions noted with justifiable bitterness although throughout history examples of contiguities being trampled to death in great conflicts were as common as were great conflicts, which, while certainly no justification, nevertheless *was a fact of political history.*

The foremost results were condemnation of the United States presence, because it was rich and powerful, and also because Communist propaganda expertise denounced the United States presence while simultaneously minimizing the actually larger but more secret DRVN presence.

Once the United States committed its troops and its Central Intelligence Agency to south-east Asia, it was too late to inaugurate a United States propaganda campaign. Further, the United States government had never correctly utilized propaganda, not even during the Second World War when informing hostile populaces of its intentions and its goals could have saved time, wealth, and lives.

The United States does not properly utilize propaganda now,

its view being both hypocritical and puritanically incorrect. Hypocritical in the sense that at least three recent Presidents, Kennedy, Johnson and Eisenhower, have lied about CIA functions, and puritanically incorrect because it considers propaganda as a variety of deliberately contrived deceit, which it certainly can be and often is, but which it most certainly does not have to be. Propaganda is a variety of national or ideological expression: whether it is honest or dishonest depends upon its inaugurators.

9

The Unconventional Conflict

French mistakes in France's former colonies of Indo-China must have established a record among modern nations for ineptitude, beginning with the slaughter of Vietnamese civilians at Cat-Bi Airfield in November of 1946 when the French cruiser *Suffern* indiscriminately shelled huddled and helpless Vietnamese refugees causing 6,000 deaths, and culminating in the senseless French humiliation at Dien Bien Phu, in May of 1954.

The eight-year French effort at reconquest, waged by a nation recently delivered from German domination by a vast Allied effort, was largely financed by the United States. Even after defeat the evacuation of French troops had to be supervised by the United States Seventh Fleet.

The Americans did not arrive in south-east Asia after the French withdrawal created the exploitable and inevitable vacuum. They had been there since 1944 and had never left. Prior to the siege at Dien Bien Phu, an established, well-entrenched United States Intelligence apparatus advised both Washington and Paris that the French would be defeated at Dien Bien Phu. Paris was outraged, but by 1954 Washington was becoming cognizant of two clear facts. The foremost fact was that Indo-China could never again be dominated by a nation as inept as France. The second fact was that, having acquiesced to French pleas for aid, and having financed the French effort at reconquest to the extent of 4,000 million dollars—on top of having spent a nearly equal amount to rehabilitate France after World War II—the surest way to waste United States money, effort, and time, was to support French arms.

United States Intelligence also reported to Washington that vast amounts of United States military aid was being secretly sold to France's enemy, the Viet-Minh, and the result of this accusation, wholly true, was that the French refused to allow American observers to enter combat zones where this multi-million dollar traffic was taking place, and a situation which had always been perplexing and became increasingly so as the United States, supporter of France, and later, of several totally corrupt and completely incompetent native Vietnamese governments, gradually became more deeply involved, not only in Vietnam but throughout all south-east Asia, until the United States commitment was total. Then, for the first time since it had become an autonomous segment of government, the Central Intelligence Agency—as had happened with its predecessor the OSS—was ordered to move into some of the areas historically reserved for conventional United States armed services, its purpose to wage the same kind of unconventional warfare the enemies of the United States were waging; the same kind of unconventional warfare the OSS had waged during the Second World War.

In Laos, for example, where invading North Vietnamese armies were operating but from which conventional United States armed forces were barred by international treaty, the CIA functioned in a twofold capacity: as an Intelligence-gathering facility, and also as a paramilitary organization. In the latter capacity its function was to engage an enemy who hoped to attack Allied forces from the rear, or from Laos into Vietnam.

The south-east Asia involvement put great strain on the CIA, particularly on its Special Operations Division. With the exception of the Soviet Union's espionage apparatus, which always had been paramilitary, most espionage establishments were not organized to conduct actual warfare. The CIA was no exception, until, by Presidential order, it was required to adapt to the exigencies then current in south-east Asia.

This fresh assignment required expansion in all areas and departments. The agency became so large that at times it was hoplessly unwieldy, a situation common among directly involved national bureaucracies in times of war.

There was also a compelling urgency. As the United States armed commitment increased, demands upon the agency became more insistent. There was great waste. There was also some success. A secret army was recruited to forestall North Vietnam's thrust, if possible, so that United States and South Vietnamese armies heavily engaged in South Vietnam would not be stabbed in the back from Laos.

This clandestine army, while outwardly commanded by General Vang Pao, was actually structured, controlled and supervised by personnel of the CIA's Special Operations Division. Its specific organizer and leader was William E. Colby, a subsequent Director of the Central Intelligence Agency, but at that time chief of the Far East Division of Clandestine Services. 'Colby's army' numbered 40,000 people, supplied, armed, and paid, by the United States through the Central Intelligence Agency, with air support provided by a CIA proprietory company, Air America, which was basically a supply, not a combat, adjunct.

Colby's '*Armée Clandestine*' bolstered the Laotian armed forces, fought Laos's own Communists, the Pathet Lao, and operated in conjunction with both United States (Allied) and South Vietnamese forces, helping very greatly to affect a situation which to a considerable degree achieved the purpose of diverting the DRVN's southerly and westerly thrusts.

All this was in violation of the 1962 Geneva Agreement, at least the *spirit* of that agreement, which forbade foreign armed forces from operating within, or from, Laos. Technically, '*L'Armée Clandestine*' was not 'foreign'. At least not at the combat level, but that, obviously, was splitting hairs. The army was a United States force in every way that mattered and the alternative to having no CIA army in Laos at that time was to imperil the Allied effort across the border in South Vietnam.

Also, the clandestine army was supported by the Laotians, and finally, North Vietnam's regular army battalions had been devastating Laos, totally ignoring its sovereignty since 1950 when the DRVN divisions under General Vo Nguyen Giap (victor over the French at Dien Bien Phu) made an abortive drive through Laos to attack Cambodia.

The DRVN's Communist Vietnamese People's Army (VPA) had an overwhelming military presence in Laos, whose embattled government solicited United States forces to counter the Communists. By the year 1964 free Laos could not have survived unless North Vietnam agreed to abide by the Geneva Agreement, and its view of those accords was evinced by the fact that immediately after ratification DRVN troops poured into Laos, openly and in contempt of the accords.

The clandestine army, whose existence was practically unrecognized during the early 1960s, operated without publicity. Nor was it as defensively oriented as were its allies in the 'other', or overt, war. Its attacks into North Vietnam were frequent, and as agency involvement grew, clandestine units operating in conjunction with ranger and commando-type units from South Vietnam as well as Laos, went north by sea, as well as by land, harassing the Communists, keeping them as much off-balance as possible, and compelling them to adopt a defensive posture in Laos in order to largely limit their effectiveness as a strike force from Laos into South Vietnam.

This CIA army employed some of the best regular and irregular troops in south-east Asia; Thai volunteers, for example, numbering close to 20,000 men. These troops, from Japan's south-east Asia ally in World War II, were redoubtable fighters. Nor were their motives entirely mercenary. Thailand, like Cambodia, was anti-Communist. Its leaders viewed the Moscow- and Peking-supported North Vietnamese armies with valid misgivings. Any Communist-dominated south-east Asian hegemony would be a direct peril to Thai independence. An exercise in pragmatic politics indicated it would be better to fight the Communists with allies, than to wait until South Vietnam, Laos and Cambodia were overrun, then make the effort alone.

The Thais had a very old military tradition. Unlike the lowland or city-dwelling Laotians, the Thais had for centuries been warlike and resolute. They at one time had a vast Asian empire, and had long employed a system requiring all male Thais to serve for a time in the armed services.

The other major source for manpower of *'L'Armée Clandestine* derived from the *'Moi'*, or hill tribesmen, the indigenous mountaineers of south-east Asia including Vietnam's *montagnards.* These people, largely insular tribesmen living apart from the lowlanders, were fiercely independent and very warlike.

Some, like the Nungs, were of Chinese origin, others were not, but whatever their ethnic origin an inhospitable and usually hostile environment had made them all independent by nature, fierce by disposition, and historically mercenary. The Rhadé, Muong, Lao, Meo tribesmen, along with their offshoots and subdivisions—all lumped together under the lowland appellation *moi*, meaning 'savage', had never been assimilated, nor was this an accident of history. Long before the French arrived south-east

Asian rulers had done nothing to educate or assimilate these people, for an excellent reason: any invader coming from the north, (originally meaning China) would have to fight these fierce tribesmen. They constituted a very respectable first line of defence.

As soldiers, generally guerrillas, they had a tradition as mercenaries. They disliked civilized lowlanders, knew their mountains better than anyone else in Laos or Vietnam, and were willing to fight for pay. For the CIA's purpose they were perfect. Also, the Communists assiduously courted them and although some fought for the DRVN the CIA's complement was very impressive, and as time passed *moi* troops of the secret army became a source of dread to the North Vietnamese.

The CIA paid them well—by their standards, but hardly ours—supplied them with beer and occasional prostitutes. It taught them the techniques of clandestine warfare. DRVN assassination teams which were an integral part of every Communist advance, were matched by *moi* teams in enemy territory. Every variety of subversion practised by the North had its counterpart in the CIA forces of the South, and as the tempo of the war increased, in scope, size, and cost, the agency's part in it correspondingly increased, both at headquarters, at Langley, Virginia, close to Washington, and overseas in south-east Asia, and yet at no time in recent history has the hired cost of mercenary soldiers been so low; as little in many cases as ten cents a day for a very capable *moi* fighting man—plus beer and other 'emoluments'.

The CIA's war, although prosecuted in conjunction with the orthodox war, and seeking identical goals, employed different methods and frequently sought different objectives. It was neither a 'tidy' nor a 'romantic' war, but the rules were not established by the United States, and while considerable subsequent acrimony was to ensue, primarily as a result of any United States presence in south-east Asia when the 'cover' was stripped from the secret war, the one being waged relentlessly by the Central Intelligence Agency, the outcry became clamorous but by that time, the late 1960s, United States taxpayers, who had never engaged in a really protracted conflict and had not been conditioned to face anything like the kinds of wars waged in Asia, were willing to accept any excuse at all which would extricate them from the heavy responsibility of supporting an effort good propagandists had convinced them could not succeed. And yet the CIA's position in south-east Asia, aside from being by order of a United States president, was no different from the identical position of the OSS in World War II, when every successful clandestine effort from assassination to plastic bombs made to resemble camel dung, had been accorded general approval.

The CIA's secret war was an *excuse* for condemnation, but it was not the *reason* for it; that went deeper, and impinged upon the fact that Americans, involved since the end of World War II in a part of the world most of them scarcely knew existed prior to World War II, having poured in an enormous fortune in money, resources, and lives, after something like eight years, were still fighting without an end in sight. *That* was the root of the United States discontent. But the CIA's war of 'dirty tricks' offered a fine example about which to profess horror and alarm. Clandestine activity at any time has been especially vulnerable.

It is not impossible that a CIA-variety war might not have succeeded in south-east Asia, although the cost in support would have been expensive and protracted. It would at least have been the kind of war Asians understood far better than they understood saturation-bombings, and great pitched battles which they systematically avoided. But the basic difference between Western-style warfare and the variety practised throughout Asia has.been that in the West awesomely overwhelming destruction has historically caused wars to end in a relatively short length of time, while in Asia, with a quite different, commonly agrarian environment, as well as a different concept of 'time' it has historically been commonplace for nations to be at war for several generations without either side having the actual capability of really destroying the economy or the ideology of the other side.

The secret war, using elements of both Eastern and Western techniques, more nearly approximated to a successful amalgam. The Laotian conflict, in which illiterate and primitive *moi* successfully stalled DRVN columns by ambush, infiltration, subversion and assassination, all the time-tested techniques of guerrilla conflict, was also prosecuted by skilled pilots of the Thai Air Force, and even more sophisticated United States pilots flying CIA aircraft, while in South Vietnam the CIA also owned another 'army', this one numbering approximately 50,000 troops. (No one knows the exact numbers, and most probably no one ever will know them; the CIA doesn't—its records were a patchwork of secrecy and bureaucratic double-talk.) This force, known as the Civilian Irregular Defence Guards, (CIDG) was another clandestine guerrilla force whose function was to wage unconventional warfare, and, as with the Laotian *Armée Clandestine*, it also co-operated with United States orthodox, or regular, units, including 'Green Berets', who were not always 'orthodox' armed elements either. CIA supervision of the specially trained CIDG ensured for South Vietnam a viable corollary comparable to the secret force in Laos, in which all the accomplishments of Asiatic-type conflict were co-ordinated with the more advanced techniques of Western warfare quite successfully.

The CIDGs, in fact, trained in terrorist tactics, were very competent jungle infiltrators, while at the same time being skilled in amphibious, commando-type raids against Communist installations, north, as well as south, of the 38th parallel. Like their Laotion counterparts, the CIDG units were capable of fielding regiment-sized attack units, and upon many occasions launched full-scale, overt operations, their ferocity and capability completely routing DRVN regular army elements. They were also supported by United States and South Vietnamese air and naval elements, and this kind of co-operative effort demoralized the Communists more consistently than did the efforts of United States and Republic of Vietnam regular (ARVN) troops.

The CIDG also served as an efficient espionage organization. Being indigenous, its members could infiltrate even Communist route-armies, rest-camps and marching DRVN columns. They could pass into North Vietnam, or appear in Viet-Cong-held areas of the South. Their value as spies was great, and except for the *moi* among them, largely Nungs, who were instantly recognizable as *moi* to other Vietnamese—if seldom to Americans or Australians—the CIDG proved to be one of the most productive and adaptable loyal forces in United States service even though at times there were instances of temperament, something predictably encounterable in any war—or, for that matter, during any peace.

A field-force of approximately one hundred thousand men, roughly divided between South Vietnam and Laos could not have won the war, obviously, even when supported by the CIA's 'air force', Air America, and its affiliates, Civil Air Transport and

Air Asia, nor with additional support from a CIA 'navy' consisting of torpedo boats and quite an assortment of other craft, but these forces were still expanding when the United States departed from south-east Asia, and unquestionably could, and in fact did, form a skilled and very effective nucleus.

CIA air armour in south-east Asia, while preponderantly of the supply category in a part of the world which is mountainous, overgrown jungle, and lacks adequate landing fields in many critical areas, also flew bombing missions.

Agency and Pentagon planners had learned lessons from the Bay of Pigs. One of them was to have control at all times of support facilities; not to be dependent upon uniformed United States armed forces which could be ordered to desist at the last moment, resulting in the abandonment of ground troops.

The number of CIA aircraft, bombers and transports numbered close to five hundred. Including pilots, bombardiers, crewmen, maintenance men, administrators and guards (as at the huge Taiwan, and Udorn, Thailand, restricted CIA air facilities) personnel of the CIA 'air force' directly involved in the support of United States and allied ground forces in South Vietnam numbered approximately 12,000 people, many of whom were highly trained aerial espionage personnel used in secret flights across hostile North Vietnam into Red China.

Thus the agency 'owned' an air force which was larger than the tactical air arms of most sovereign nations, as well as an army which, if not as large, was as well equipped, supplied and supported, as many national armies, and for the kind of combat it was trained to engage in, was also superior to many armies.

There was also a CIA 'navy', but because the nature of the conflict would clearly not be resolved, nor to any appreciable degree influenced or decided by naval action, this force was negligible. Also, CIA commando-type raids up the coast into Viet-Cong controlled territory, or even into North Vietnam itself, were not mounted with a view to affecting permanent bases, even though some were, in fact, affected to land infiltrators who did not retire, but who remained within enemy territory to operate as terrorist teams.

The vessels used in these operations, CIA controlled and originally of United States manufacture, were in general the property of the South Vietnamese navy and were of the torpedo-boat class, heavily armoured—and armed—but designed to rely more on speed than fire-power.

They operated extensively along hostile coastlines, but except when entering DRVN territorial waters, where they were frequently challenged by the North Vietnamese navy, there was actually little danger of interception or sinking—particularly since most raids were undertaken by night when the effectiveness of enemy shore batteries was limited.

As the war continued, agency air and land involvement steadily expanded. For example, the Air America-Air Asia consortium broadened in base and scope until a veritable armada of aircraft dominated the skies of south-east Asia, in size and firepower far superior to anything the DRVN could match, and this was not taking into account the even more formidable United States Air Force, which was almost totally tactical.

In fact, CIA proprietories were so busy supplying and spying that overlapping responsibilities often made it necessary for pilots to carry two sets of identification symbols. When they landed upon the completion of one mission, logged as having been flown for one proprietory, while their aircraft were being serviced and reloaded, they stripped off one set of identifying letters and numbers, replacing them with another set to be used in the ensuing flight. Keeping exact records would have been a challenge under most normal conditions. In war, and being part of a clandestine operation, made the keeping of records impossible and of course, in many instances, there were obvious reasons for not attempting to keep records at all.

By the time United States overt participation in Vietnam ceased, the Central Intelligence Agency was operating successfully in almost all areas, and since the nature of this conflict was admirably suited to clandestine activity, after the official withdrawal of United States forces, the agency continued active—and still does—but the forces of reaction in the United States, having finally undertaken an investigation of such CIA phases as funding, secret commitments, and undercover conduct, it would appear that, although most certainly *all* support of the embattled free nations of south-east Asia would not end, to a considerable extent overt support would end, including some CIA participation.

Those who had doubts that any secret function could be terminated because by its nature when exposed or threatened it simply goes underground, might well bear in mind that even the most sophisticated and elusive secret operation is dependent upon funds. Limit the funding, and all the subterfuge in the world will not prevent curtailment of clandestine activity.

10

Some Aspects of a Dilemma

For the Central Intelligence Agency, south-east Asia became a spectre which would not go away. The executive branch of government was subject to change, by law and politics, every four years, from president and secretary of state on down, and normally with the departure of these people went their accountability, but the professionals in government were still there, saddled with the implementation of the decisions and judgements, good or bad, of those who had departed.

United States presidents from Harry Truman to Dwight Eisenhower. John Kennedy, Lyndon Johnson and Richard Nixon, favoured a strong stance of militancy in south-east Asia, and right or wrong as each departed his legacy and its implementation lingered.

In south-east Asia the United States fought as a result of a commitment to an ally, the Republic of South Vietnam. In Laos, where there were not supposed to be any foreign armed forces, the secret army was in place because the president of the United States, the secretary of state, the joint chiefs of staff, the National Security Council, and many members of the legislative branch of government approved of its operation in the surest of all ways to evince approval—by funding it.

The greatest difficulties arose when all those elected officials and their appointed functionaries, such as Secretaries of State John Foster Dulles and Dean Rusk, left office, having resolved very little during their tenure except the hard fact that the CIA was to continue functioning in the future as it had in the past, meaning that it was to press the clandestine war in Laos as vigorously as ever, and in other areas was to function as it still does, according to the orders and the edicts of officials who have since departed from the halls of power, and also by the direction their successors, men who failed to grasp the significance of how seriously change had eroded the political philosophies of several spectres—Eisenhower, Kennedy, Johnson—and the philosophies of several yet existing anachronisms—Allen Dulles and Dean Rusk—and one blackguard, Richard Nixon.

From this situation came the denunciation of CIA activities, as though the agency were a sovereign entity deserving exclusive blame. The idolators who extolled a martyred John Kennedy were the same people who decried CIA activities—which could only have been undertaken with President Kennedy's approval, and by his executive order.

In Laos, the actual success of many CIA undertakings was largely obscured by the war in South Vietnam which took precedent, and also because the Laotian involvement was kept as secret as the CIA's best efforts towards that end could keep it. But the entire Laotian affair was embarked upon and prosecuted with *executive knowledge*.

Not general public knowledge, and perhaps not—in its fullest extent—with total Congressional knowledge, but with the support of every major United States official in the executive branch, the Department of State, and the major executives of the administrative arm of government.

The eerie aspect was how little the United States electorate, and the world in general, ever really learned about the CIA's Laotian operation.

In a nation where freedom of the press had been so arduously defended, investigative reporting, strident though it was—and abrasive though it remains—accomplished a failure of major proportions.

The Central Intelligence Agency, with its private army, its private air force, was actually and successfully waging a war, and at home in the United States as well as overseas in London and Berlin, the news-conscious general public had scarcely an inkling.

The identity of the chief architect of this secret war was even less known, and although subsequent agency director William Colby, without question one of the best administrators then in government, had a colourful past in espionage, including secret service in German-occupied France and Norway during World War II, until his appointment as CIA director in early September of 1973, even the press hardly had heard of him.

In Vietnam, he was also the organizer of the Provincial Reconnaissance Units programme (PRU), whose original designation, Counter Terror, was quickly changed, but which more nearly described the function of those specially trained troops whose emulation of, and improvement upon, DRVN tactics included infiltration of Communist areas for purposes of disruption, intimidation, abduction and murder, as well as the maintenance of interrogation posts where confessions, admissions, and Intelligence information was extracted by PRU Vietnamese cadres from Viet-Cong and DRVN captives.

Another Colby innovation was the 'Phoenix' programme, inaugurated in 1967 throughout South Vietnam. Its purpose was the elimination of Communist spies, assassins, and terrorists who had made life increasingly hazardous in the countryside as well as in the hamlets and cities.

The success of 'Phoenix' was undeniable; it cost the Viet-Cong more than 20,000 casualties in its first thirty months of operation, and because at the countryside level it was administered by the Vietnamese, who employed the same techniques used by the Provincial Reconnaissance Units, it was callous, brutal, and included physical torture as well as perfunctory execution.

By 1967 William Colby was in charge of a new programme, this one aimed at anti-corruption and pacification. The purpose was to devise methods which would result in the strengthening of South Vietnam's economy, compel a reduction of corruption in government, and also to encourage a more wholehearted support of the Thieu régime throughout South Vietnam.

The effort to end corruption was doomed before it was undertaken. There was no more corrupt government on earth than that of South Vietnam. The effort to win the people of South Vietnam to President Thieu's support by appeals to all social and political factions, did not succeed either, primarily because Nguyen Van Thieu was himself indifferent to it. He evinced no interest in any support not deriving from his army or the United States Treasury.

Nevertheless, William Colby, whose versatility enabled him to field-marshal a successful army in Laos, to inaugurate terrorism as an answer to terrorism, and to administer programmes whose purpose was to heal and placate remained largely a little-known enigma to Americans and to Europeans.

If, as has been posited, his talents were ambiguous, so, it might also be said, was his environment in both the seats of power, at home in the United States, and in south-east Asia. So, in fact, was —and is—the total ambience and while ambiguities proliferate and social philosophers endlessly equivocate, nations and ideologies, but most importantly of all, freedom itself, can die.

Vietnam was an immense meat-grinder into which was fed a steady dribble of sacrificial victims from half-a-dozen countries, and behind the scenes the secret machinations on both sides kept pace, their amorality not in the least off-key from the total sordid orchestrations. This did not make them morally or ethically correct, but they were integral elements of the same chaotic ambience which was not of the CIA's creation despite the accusations of denunciatory dissenters worldwide whose anguished outcries for cessation seemed never to extend quite as far as the Communist side, where the greatest proportion of outrages were committed.

Nevertheless, secret wars, like conventional ones, phase out only very slowly, and in fact the secret variety of conflict has a capacity for endurance orthodox conflicts seldom possess.

They enjoy the distinction of covert intrigue, as well as a dogged resilience. In Laos, for example, although with the installation of a Laotian coalition government including Communist Pathet Lao representatives, much of the hostility ultimately ended and the CIA officially withdrew from the country in late June of 1973, in fact General Vang Pao, the agency's commander in the north, retained his position as the Meo warlord and remained in CIA pay.

When Vang Pao's army was disbanded and roughly half of it was incorporated into the regular Laotian army, at a lower rate of pay, and more of it was sent back to the highland farming villages to resume a normal agrarian existence (growing opium, among other crops), also at a reduced standard of living, the alternatives appeared to be brigandage, or additional service for the CIA in different circumstances.

In the province of Xieng Khouang, for example, secret agency funding presently supports a large number of hill-tribesmen, formerly cadremen of *L'Armée Clandestine*, through a number of agricultural projects. Justification for this programme is premised on the possibility of a fresh outbreak of hostilities in Laos, in which event the secret army could, within a very short space of time, be re-activated.

As such programmes go this one is quite inexpensive. In fact, there is an excellent opportunity that, as a result of United States Agency for International Development (AID) supervision, it could not only become self-supporting, it could ultimately become self-sustaining and in fact, profitable.

Also, again illuminating the way conflicts have been historically conducted in Asia, in Xieng Khouang the province of General Vang Pao, the secretly funded pig, chicken, and cattle farms support tribesmen who are still the troops of a respected warlord. Profits from the CIA-funded 'Xieng Khouang Development Association' help Vang Pao buy the loyalty and support of other highland warlords.

Anachronistic as it appears, nonetheless that is how it works. But many tribesmen have neither accepted incorporation into the regular Laotian army, nor resettlement. Roughly a month after the CIA officially withdrew from Laos, and its secret army cadremen were to end hostilities and relinquish their modern United States weapons, a band of men ambushed a bus travelling between Vientiane and the royal capital of Luang Prabang, opened fire with United States M16 rifles, and killed two Australian passengers, the sister-in-law, and the brother of the Australian ambassador to Laos.

Other similar occurrences, dozens of them in fact, have been blamed on the ready availability of abandoned United States weapons, or those secretly cached by the hill people who were supposed to have surrendered them, and while the CIA was in no way responsible for the death of the Alexander Borthwicks in the July bus-ambush, the fact is that this incident and many others are some aspects of the continuing south-east Asia dilemma.

It would be nice if an understandable explanation to the dilemma of south-east Asia were possible. At least Western minds would then be able rationally to arrive at Western-type judgements, but there exists no such explanation, and those who attempt clear-cut delineations commit a deliberate disservice.

Not for the past generation, or roughly about the time of the initial direct United States and Allied (Australian, United Nations, British and French) involvement, has it been possible to present a rational view of Indo-china. For example, subsequent to World

War II, Nationalist Chinese troops, allies of the war's anti-Fascist powers, of which Free France was one, disarmed and interned the Free French forces of General Sabbatier, while everyone's enemy, Japan's Thirty-eighth Area Army, 50,000 strong, under Count Terauchi, was *not* disarmed, and was used to patrol Indo-china and maintain prison camps where French and other Allied troops languished, and the commander of Chiang Kai-shek's anti-Communist Nationalist Chinese troops, General Lu-han, served the Red Chinese, and the Americans under General Wedemeyer tried to oppose both the British and the French while simultaneously funding and supporting Hanoi's Communists under Ho Chi Minh.

That was thirty years ago, and conceivably conditions could have stabilized during the interim. Instead, if possible, they became even more incomprehensible.

Vietnam became a charnal house. So did Laos, until coalescence brought about a measure of uncertain order, but what actually occurred in Laos, as the Central Intelligence Agency discovered, was that with a very unstable truce established in 1973 in a country whose people were apathetically numb from war, was that the Communists began at once to use Laos as exactly the staging area they had intended to use it as before *L'Armée Clandestine* upset that scheme.

With the secret army officially disbanded, Laos became the funnel for arms and men south from North Vietnam to the battlefields, cities, lowlands, highlands, and rice paddies of South Vietnam. But also a fresh implementation to a very old plan was undertaken : a Communist thrust against Cambodia, where it had not been entirely feasible to deliver Communist troops and weaponry before—when the CIA's secret army in Laos had been available and willing to stem that flow—was undertaken.

Cambodia, while obviously geographically involved in whatever occurred in Indo-china—south-east Asia—managed until 1964 to maintain a relatively neutral posture, in part because its neutrality had been guaranteed by the United States and South Vietnam who had agreed to protect it, and partly because, although it possessed a Cambodian Communist Party, (the Kmer Rouge) the Reds were neither strong nor especially aggressive prior to 1964.

Cambodia was therefore certain to benefit from the south-east

Asian war. It was distant from North Vietnam. It had two embattled contiguities, Laos and South Vietnam between it and the Communist peril. It was also adjacent to the tough, resourceful, strongly militant anti-Communist Thais. Then, in July of 1964, this situation began subtly to change, with the Communists achieving control (control in this context meaning at least ninety per cent of local support) below Saigon, in South Vietnam, southerly and westerly, including the region of the Camau Peninsula close to the border below Phnon Penh in Cambodia, and a widening war began to imperil Cambodia's 'favoured nation' status.

That same year, 1964, the Communists in Laos overran half the nation on down the spiny border and inland to the Cambodian border. At this time Cambodia, under its unstable Prince Norodom Sihanouk, had a 30,000-man army, a small navy and a small air force. The Central Intelligence Agency, like the oldtime OSS which had preceded it into Cambodia during and subsequent to World War II, had an established station in the country, but lacked both power and influence; no one had evidently thought, prior to 1964, that Cambodia would become an actual battleground.

The country abruptly became a DRVN sanctuary. Communists and DRVN regular troops came across the border in droves. Cambodia asked the United Nations Security Council to guarantee its neutrality. The UN fearful of direct involvement in what had by 1964 become a war nearly as total as the recent one in Europe, World War II, offered to send an 'Observer Force' but otherwise declined to intervene.

The Communists increased their espionage and terrorists cadres in Cambodia. Vacillating Prince Sihanouk performed a belated *volte face*, visited Peking, called Red China his ally and the United States Cambodia's imperialist enemy, and the unravelling of neutraliy moved swiftly towards a *dénouement*, a perhaps inevitable situation since the embattled Allies in South Vietnam were then faced, not simply with a neutralized Laos from which the Communists were increasingly infiltrating across the border, but also by a fresh peril, a Communist Cambodia, from which additional Communists (Kmer Rouge—'Red' Kmer, or Cambodians) could conceivably also cross into southern South Vietnam from the central highlands to actually behind and below Saigon.

They could, in fact, control the Mekong estuary, which was Saigon's lifeline.

The CIA's role was clear-cut. Prince Sihanouk had to go. A pro-American Cambodian named Lon Nol mounted a successful *coup* in 1970, Prince Norodom Sihanouk was overthrown and ousted, but, as in all aspects of the south-east Asia dilemma, this removed a thorn from United States flesh, but by no means uprooted the entire bush. In fact the overthrow of Sihanouk did exactly what the United States had sought to avoid. It strengthened the Kmer Rouge. Thousands of uncommitted Cambodians, sensing a foreign hand—and CIA's—in the Lon Nol success, and antagonized by this, flocked to join the Kmer Rouge.

Another factor which aided the Communists occurred two months later, when President Nixon ordered the invasion of Cambodia. From a neutral United States protectorate Cambodia now became another charnel house, with more outraged Cambodians joining the Kmer Rouge, and the irony was that although the Kmer Rouge was Communist at the core, by late 1970 it had more nationalist Cambodians than hard-line Communists in its ranks.

President Nixon's invasion order was to have the most sanguinary results, and while one element of it—for United States forces to find and capture North Vietnam's 'Central Office for South Vietnam', the secret co-ordinating war-council of Hanoi—failed, (COSV was never found) other results were more murkily spectacular, including a bombing war which was deliberately undertaken in secret and kept from the United States public.

The CIA was involved from the beginning, but political and tactical blunders, one upon the heels of the other, came so fast there was no time to create more than a weak nucleus of another secret army. Nor was this a CIA failure. Responsibility lay almost exclusively with both the executive and administrative sectors of the United States government.

Finally, when the second 'secret war' came to public view in the United States the outcry was tumultuous. This was to result in some twenty university campus riots, including the one at Kent State University in Ohio where National Guardsmen shot into a mob of rioting students. It also resulted in making public the 'Pentagon Papers', a harrowing exposé of United States foreign policy in south-east Asia.

The CIA's position in Cambodia was almost passive, once Lon Nol was seated as Chief of State. Cambodia became and remained a Pentagon problem. For the Central Intelligence Agency there had not been time enough to organize another *Armée Clandestine*, and President Nixon's blunder was, in fact, deplored by the agency leadership, and if some Special Operations personnel and those in Clandestine Services were willing to become involved, others clearly were not, and not entirely because Cambodia was an unwinnable situation. A petition opposing the Cambodian venture on moral grounds was circulated, and signed, by so many agency people that then-Director Richard Helms called several high-level conferences in an effort to achieve some kind of amelioration. Never before in agency history had there been a rebellion.

Ultimately, the near-rebellion was quashed, but no one, including the directors who succeeded Helms, could tranquilly believe that because of an oath to maintain secrecy and to support the policies of the United States, there did not exist a degree of morality within the agency.

Meanwhile, the south-east Asian quagmire continued to plague the CIA as it did every other area of government and politics, and when all the gunfire ended, agency espionage activity remained strong and active. South-east Asia was a window towards Red China, a gateway to the North Pacific and Indian Ocean communities of nations, and a point of observation—and detection—of Communism's certain attempts at expansion towards Indonesia and on southward towards Australia. But the accumulation of Intelligence was not the same as 'owning' armies and air forces, and conducting overt warfare. These latter things were the result of outmoded statescraft, and they deserved to be changed at the level of the Department of State, the Executive and Congressional levels. Otherwise nothing could prevent what resulted from the south-east Asian dilemma—a huge, unwieldly, appallingly expensive, pre-emptive Central Intelligence Agency with the power to intervene in any situation it was ordered into by those whose power employed the agency as a paramilitary establishment.

11

The Octopus's Shadow

A declining role for the Central Intelligence Agency in south-east Asia did not mean its clandestine activity there was at an end. It meant that its total south-east Asian function could be curtailed, but the agency remained—and still remains—entrenched: 'in place'.

Its support of a respectable infrastructure continued, but the old paramilitary role passed, which, in some respects, insured a more costly and less 'winnable' war for South Vietnam and its allies.

The CIA Laotian affair was an example of how using Communist multi-faceted strategy and tactics against Communists, could succeed. If the United States, instead of reverting to the bankrupting, Western style, World War II variety of force—then doing so with one arm tied behind its back—had supported a dozen indigenous 'Colby's armies', victory would have been entirely feasible, the war would have had less the appearance of foreign intervention' it subsequently had, and although it would have dragged on and on, it would have cost a fraction of what it did cost.

However, with the phasing-out of the Laotian affair, the assumption by the orthodox military of all aspects of the war, the agency, which had grown astonishingly as a result of its south-east Asian commitment, did not revert. Government agencies, even those lacking the capacity for self-perpetuating malignancy most bureaucracies possess, having once achieved an eminence, do not gracefully relinquish that eminence, and the CIA after south-east Asia was a true monolith. Its authorized personnel limit of roughly 18,000 people and a one billion dollar annual budget, actually only reflected the tip of the iceberg. It still possessed proprietary aircraft companies, entire corps of secret agents—

'consultants'—large, established subsidiary espionage and clandestine operations offices requiring entire high-rise buildings to house them in such places as West Berlin (its largest European affiliate), London, and the Middle East. It owned ships, fleets of cars, even valuable blocks of industrial and residential property. There was no individual in the world, even including those within the Soviet Union, who did not exist in the shadow of the CIA octopus, no aspect of the social, technological, cultural or educational human experience was not under that shadow. Those who claimed otherwise could never have been more incorrect.

After its curtailed participation in operations in south-east Asia, the agency, monolithic in size, tremendously international in scope, the most powerful Intelligence operation ever possessed in the West, had spies 'in place' in the Soviet Union, as elsewhere, and the contention that 'closed societies' had inherent safeguards against foreign espionage penetration was nothing more than the normal reaction of denigration used by all Intelligence operations to obscure a secret. The CIA monitored actual conversations of Soviet leaders while riding in their State limousines in Moscow, (and learned whose back ached today, and whose other homely complaints were a source of minor grievance among the Soviet leadership).

It has been customary in recent years to maintain the fiction that only through spy-in-the-sky satellites has the United States and its allies been able to determine Soviet military strength, and from analyses of these viewings to make accurate prognostications of the USSR's potential.

It has also been somewhat disparagingly noted (again, Marks and Marchetti), that the occasional fluke, such as the defection of Colonel Oleg Penkovskiy, Russian war hero, has been the CIA's second best source of Intelligence from within the USSR, after satellite overflights.

Satellite detection and an occasional valuable defection are enormously contributory to the agency's vast secret knowledge of the Soviet Union as well as of all other nations, but regardless of the recurrent theme that individual espionage penetration is *passé* in the 1970s, it remains the best source of information about internal Cuba, East Germany, China, and the Soviet Union. Many of the agency's recent penetration programmes have been successful because of a good balance between technological techniques and its other source of covert Intelligence, the common spy. He—or she—provides information satellites cannot provide. He—or she—is also more productive year in-year out than defectors, and operates in positions where technology is no substitute for human judgment.

Two particular sectors of the agency, the Directorate of Intelligence and the Directorate of Operations have been especially concerned with espionage penetration, but other elements have also been both involved and contributory. Nor has this aspect of the Intelligence function been aimed exclusively at establishing agents in foreign lands. At both agency headquarters in Langley, Virginia, and the secret training facility near historic Williamsburg in south-eastern Virginia, Camp Peary, an ostensible military research facility, United States policemen were trained in phases of detection, control, containment, dispersion and apprehension, while at the same time the agency's primary interest, being espionage, these and other secret bases in the United States, in Latin America, and also in Europe, were used for the preparation of spies, in accordance with the agency's continuing large-scale operation after the nearly total curtailment of its south-east Asia commitment.

For example, not long ago when Thailand's Prime Minister Sirit Thanarat was hospitalized in Tokyo, members of an opposition group seized upon his absence from Thailand to undertake a *coup*. CIA agents detected early warnings of the trouble, sent an aeroplane to Japan for the Prime Minister, and simultaneously activated CIA-trained Thai loyalists, and when Sirit Thanarat arrived in Bangkok, with a party of skilled bodyguards who were also CIA-trained, the *coup* collapsed.

CIA-trained troops constituted Thailand's palace guard. This force as well as Thai Intelligence units which had also been trained by the Central Intelligence Agency, comprised an excellent source of information. Commander of the palace guard, General Vitoon Yasawad, was also commander of Thailand's secret army units in Laos. He had the reputation of being absolutely dependable, and had long been in the employment of the agency.

Cynics could with some justification claim that this kind of a situation actually amounted to a variety of 'palace captivity' for Thailand's royal family.

It also happened to be the best kind of protection for Thailand's rulers and political leaders in a part of the world and at a time when the largely discredited 'domino theory' of falling nations in south-east Asia could be implemented through a series of assassinations which could encourage Thailand to follow Laos and Cambodia behind the Communists' bamboo curtain.

The élite corps responsible for the protection of leaders in many lands, including Jordan, South Korea, Indonesia, South Vietnam, plus a number of countries in the Middle East, Africa, and Latin America, are CIA-trained.

The advantages to any Intelligence service, of 'in place' foreign recruits is obvious, and while palace guards and the security agents of many lands have been courted for centuries (England's Sir Francis Walsingham used them repeatedly to save the life of Queen Elizabeth I from the assassins of Spain's Philip II and the Jesuits, four centuries ago) there has in modern times been another, and greater source of recruits : the police.

Every year dozens of nations have sent candidates from their police establishments to the United States for specialized training. Many of these men have been recruited.

Director William Colby has acknowledged that this practice has been largely successful. Foreign police are usually in a position to provide information at a level palace guards and secret internal officials at the political-diplomatic level are not involved with.

The agency's exploitation of this source of spies encouraged it to provide financial support for the International Police Academy, in Washington, where approximately 7,000 foreign police have received instruction over the past dozen years from 75 countries.

The academy is an overt adjunct of the United States Agency for International Development (AID) which, up to the year 1965, had contributed $22 billion to developing nations, the great proportion of which was advanced for agricultural, industrial, and commercial projects.

Nevertheless, it has been clearly stated what AID's aims are : 'to promote world conditions which will permit this nation [the United States] to survive, to progress, and to prosper, in a setting of peace and [with] its fundamental human values safely secured'. In clear language AID is for the purpose of helping those in need of technical and financial assistance in such relevant fields as agriculture, commerce and industry, in foreign lands, and in helping the United States Intelligence establishment at home.

One of AID's programmes, under the heading of 'Public Safety Division', was involved with the training of foreign police at AID's International Police Academy. The CIA connection was never publicized, but neither, apparently, was it very abstruse, because at least one United States Senator, James Abourezk, a Democrat of South Dakota, managed to uncover it at a time (1975) when one of the surest ways to achieve minor-celebrity status was to appear as a CIA witch-hunter.

Actually, the CIA-IPA connection was dissolved in either 1973 or 1974, with CIA support withdrawn, which, while a salve to some senatorial and congressional consciences, need not mean much. Intelligence 'case officers', those to whom recruited spies report, can very easily procure names of possible additional recruits from their foreign Intelligence sources.

Also, there has recently developed in the United States an institution known as the National Intelligence Academy (NIA). It is located in the perpetual-summer land of Fort Lauderdale, Florida. It is owned by a private individual named Leo Goodwin, an ageing former paratrooper whose vast fortune derives from the insurance business. Goodwin has spent $1 million annually since 1972 creating NIA, and has succeeded in establishing probably the best privately owned Intelligence facility in the world. Police from many lands have been enrolled at a flat rate of $760 per individual for courses that cover utilization of the latest and most sophisticated electronics surveillance equipment. Courses are also given in national and international law, in the use of night-vision equipment, listening devices, and the application of all manner of detection equipment.

The NIA is operated as a non-profit establishment, which has certain taxation advantages, and while its director, Ronald Stanley, has emphatically denied a CIA connection, it is also a fact that among NIA's personnel there have been former CIA agents, and it is also a fact that agents from another federal agency, the Secret Service, have evinced professional interest in the National Intelligence Academy.

If the NIA has superseded the International Police Academy as a source of espionage recruits, which is almost a certainty, there is another connection which may ultimately cause embarrassment.

In NIA's Fort Lauderdale headquarters another private company which deals in electronic espionage instruments, called the 'Audio Intelligence Devices Company', is ostensibly owned and operated by a man named Jack Holcomb (on whom British West Indies Intelligence has a dossier) who, while denying an affiliation with the NIA, did in fact co-operate with Leo Goodwin in establishing the NIA, and has served as an unofficial NIA consultant.

If the National Intelligence Academy can be discredited, it can probably be done through the Goodwin-Holcomb relationship. As for an NIA-CIA connection, it undoubtedly exists, but otherwise the NIA, while naturally preferring anonymity, is not an illegal or a clandestine operation. It has thus far trained police, usually plainclothes or undercover, agents, (something the Federal Bureau of Investigation has been doing for decades with a minimum of outcry) from thirty states and at least four foreign nations, with negotiations in progress with another dozen foreign nations.

The NIA is only the latest source for Central Intelligence Agency recruitment. For more than twenty years the agency was involved with an alleged private company in Washington called 'International Police Services, Incorporated', which in fact was wholly CIA dominated, and which also trained the police of several states within the United States, as well as foreign police. International Police Services also offered a post-graduate course for police trained elsewhere, furnishing equipment, much of it technical surveillance and detection apparatus, which went back to foreign countries with the officers trained in its use.

These things were only a small part of the diversification and broadened scope of Central Intelligence Agency activity made possible once the south-east Asian commitment was curtailed and while the funding and expansion of the agency remained at the Laos level.

Secret training bases from Panama to Iran to West Germany and England, flourished, and although the agency's private tactical air force was largely in mothballs (in Arizona), its proprietary commercial air lines continued to operate, and still do, with some of them, like Intermountain Aviation, Air Asia, Southern Air Transport and Air America, actually making profits as commercial carriers.

Also, covert penetration was accelerated. Labour unions in France, West Germany, Great Britain, and Scandinavia were infiltrated. Youth movements, political parties, even many commercial companies with valuable contracts, as well as industrial manufacturing companies, even fishing fleets and the union organizations associated with them, were penetrated. Agency wealth, plus size, made possible the kind of espionage by a facility in the West equal to that of the Soviet Union's hydra-headed espionage establishment.

Youth movements around the world have for obvious reasons been a particular target of penetration by all Intelligence establishments, and it has frequently happened that British, French, Soviet and United States agents and paid informers have not only penetrated these groups, but have also funded them. The same condition applies with respect to labour unions. In fact the CIA has funded anti-American movements within foreign labour unions in order to facilitate penetration and manipulation.

Education, which for many years was almost an exclusive Soviet Intelligence target, became a source of CIA interest even before the 1960s, which was the decade most noted for worldwide campus unrest over the past thirty years. In this field the agency funded activist groups, bought vocal, often radical leaders, and at the academic level moved to discredit instructors whose political philosophies were leftist, while at the same time 'subsidizing' professors whose leanings were either centrist or right of centre.

Within the United States CIA activity was never as outright nor as widespread as it was outside the country, and in fact, although it was subsequently to be alleged that agency violation of its charter in this respect was blatantly uninhibited, this was not true, and for an elemental reason : America's enemies within the country were nowhere nearly as numerous as they were outside the country.

However, charges of spying within the United States would inevitably proliferate, exactly as they would throughout the world, which was one of the prices the agency was obliged to pay for having become so large. Dozens of the most illogical allegations were charged against the agency. It became an almost natural reflex to lay blame against the CIA, and such were the ironies of this condition that when the President of Mexico was shouted down at a university in Mexico in March of 1975, when he finally was driven from the speaker's rostrum, he denounced the students as CIA-inspired dupes. In former times they would have been Communist dupes.

There were handicaps to size. They had become apparent in Vietnam and Laos. Efficiency suffered, the quality of personnel deteriorated, and bureaucratic sclerosis occurred along with poor craftsmanship. Also, there was duplication of effort as well as an overlapping of functions between the agency and several other Intelligence-gathering establishments such as the FBI, particularly with respect to internal, United States covert activity.

Still, the nature of the CIA prevented it from becoming another moribund State Department, and that at least was in its favour.

Otherwise, though, size and wealth offered opportunities for greater espionage activity, along with opportunities for penetration and manipulation on a scale never before attempted by a United States Intelligence organization, as in Greece, where John Maury, later Legislative Counsel for the agency, was for many years chief of station—or supreme United States Intelligence executive. But this identical size and power possessed within itself the germs of Monolithic Disease, i.e., when a bureaucracy becomes so large and so powerful that its activities irritate too many people, the reaction can be violently antagonistic which was what had happened to the Central Intelligence Agency by 1974–75. Even its friends had become chary and the shadow of an octopus could be fatal—to the octopus.

12

Control Organizations

It is axiomatic that the size and the wealth of a bureaucracy can ensure its entrenched position providing it possesses even a remotely valid reason for existence. It is also axiomatic that a bureaucracy as powerful as the Central Intelligence Agency can survive investigations and attempts at stringent control through the employment of its uniquely professional expertise in penetrating and ultimately controlling such organizations, and uneasy as this fact of life may make many people, it is not necessarily a bad thing.

A strictly bureaucratic CIA would be useless; if the day arrived when the Intelligence function were reduced to simple analysis and theoretical prognostication it would mark the end of a genuine Free World Intelligence function and the beginning of a fatally moribund, redundant bureaucratic function. If the CIA were totally under the control of non-Intelligence-oriented politicians, its value would end.

Nevertheless, controls are desirable, otherwise the kind of rampant espionage which allowed the agency to violate its National Security Act charter of 1947, and engage in espionage within the United States, would proliferate—as, in fact, happened.

The danger in any Intelligence operation arises when *all* control-committee members think alike—in a way which favours the recommendations of an Intelligence community. Fortunately, this condition rarely occurs, perhaps as a result of so many different kinds of people being involved, whose political and social philosophies are so inevitably varied.

Nevertheless, during crisis conditions such as the recently concluded south-east Asian experience, political—or emotional—influences can, and in fact *have*, upset the system of requisite checks and balances in a way which has resulted in the support of entire sequences of bad decisions, and those committeemen whose inherent reluctance should have encouraged them to protest or at least to have abstained, were carried along by a highly skilled, erudite and eloquent corps of Intelligence-community cadremen, with some very questionable results.

How this was achieved in the past was exemplified by a National Security Council directive which allowed the CIA to interrogate US citizens who had returned from overseas sojourns. In itself, this was a harmless procedure, even though it technically violated the 1947 charter which forbade any police-type activity. But it was only one step from harmlessly engaging American travellers in a polite questioning procedure, to engaging in secret investigations of these same people, and from there, indulging in all the classical espionage-investigative procedures which included compiling dossiers on private individuals.

How could it happen? Very simply: despite the prohibitive controls entailed in the 1947 charter, subsequent, and secret, National Security Council directives which were not made public (still have not been made public) permitted certain abrogations which broadened the base and expanded the power of the Intelligence-investigative operation, and, as has been demonstrated countless times with respect to other bureaucracies, the Central Intelligence Agency simply accrued to itself more and more power.

The National Security Council, which was established in 1947 and whose regulatory position was mentioned in Chapter Two, was *not* to be CIA-controlled. In fact the council was to evaluate information provided by the Intelligence sector, and the CIA was to 'perform . . . as the National Security Council may from time to time direct'. Originally, the council was to direct the agency, not the other way around.

At roughly the same time another regulatory, or at least a supposedly supervisory, organization was created. The Office Of Policy Co-ordination, (OPC). The function of the OPC was to evaluate Intelligence and report, not to the Director of the CIA, but rather to the Departments of State and Defence. There was, however, a close link between OPC and the CIA. Further, OPC's chief was Frank Wisner Jr, a former wartime OSS agent, Intelligence-oriented and paramilitary-minded. Subsequently, when consolidation of Intelligence-evaluation agencies was promulgated under agency director General Walter Bedell Smith, the OPC was swallowed whole, and re-emerged, with Frank Wisner second-in-command, as part of the CIA's Office Of Special Operations, while the National Security Council, which could hardly be cannibalized as the OPC had been, some of its members having Cabinet-rank, while others were highly influential at Army, Navy, and State Department levels, was directly CIA-influenced, one of its members, Henry Kissinger, being notably Intelligence-minded and usually hawkish, while another member, the CIA's director, served as Presidential adviser. The result was that, despite the earlier intention of President Truman that the council control the agency, by the year 1969 the tail was wagging the dog, not the other way around, a condition which still exists.

It was unavoidable, then, that the fine line which the British had warned about—Intelligence formulating national policy—obtained. The National Security Council, founded to control the agency, was ultimately controlled by the agency, but of equal gravity was an innovation which arose from Henry Kissinger's view that immediate problems—surface tensions—were more important than historic perspectives. Out of this fresh position arose an approach based only peripherially upon Intelligence, and more upon the old-line US position of approaching foreign problems with a blank cheque in hand.

The results of emulating ancient Byzantium's largesse has been generally the same for the United States and Dr Kissinger as they were for Byzantium and the Comneni : initial success and ultimate failure. Any short-term view of world problems involving only financial salve rarely improves bad situations except temporarily. Sound Intelligence, basic *facts* arising from historic perspectives, are more likely to ensure success, but even then success at the diplomatic level is enormously elusive.

When the National Security Council became a Kissinger implement to be used in the day-to-day shuttling of a sincere but depthless innovative diplomat, rather than an organization aspect control of the Central Intelligence Agency, it ceased to serve even the spirit of its founding concept. But one little-recognized aspect of the Kissinger-NSC association emerged, which was certain to find favour within the Intelligence system : Secretary of State Henry Kissinger, as head of the National Security Council, also became tacit head of the CIA, a unique situation in that CIA influence over the Council had succeeded so well that the Council's chief not only abetted CIA influence but ultimately also directed and implemented it.

Another supposed control organization was the so-called '40 Committee', which was established in the early days of CIA activity to monitor agency covert activities, and presumably, exert control over zealous agency directors as well as functionaries. The committee was to serve secretly. Its panel consisted of an Under Secretary of State, a Deputy Director of Defence, the current Chairman of the Joint Chiefs of Staff, plus a number of prominent politicians and lesser augmentary personnel—plus the director of the CIA.

This organization was also known by other names. Each time its existence was exposed a fresh name was adopted, among them were the 303 Committee, Special Group, 40 Committee, *et al*, but it was for thirty years the actual formulator of United States foreign policy, and it was dominated in its later years by two men, the Director of the CIA and Dr Henry Kissinger. In fact, it was this committee which advocated United States involvement in the Chilean Allende affair, previously mentioned, which occurred in the early 1970s.

The 40 Committee, like the National Security Council, was penetrated early and was subsequently dominated by the CIA, whose director (Richard Helms during the Allende affair) officiated at convened conferences.

In theory the 40 Committee met four times a month, but in actuality a full convention only obtained if there was a critical issue at stake. Members of the committee were essentially the same as for the National Security Council; a Deputy Director of Defence, an Under Secretary of State, Chairman of the Joint Chiefs, and Henry Kissinger, who, in former times, sat in as a presidential adviser.

Both the 40 Committee and the National Security Council reported to the United States President, and neither was authorized to employ unilateral action, nor did they—nor did they have to; once a popular decision was arrived at, each United States President from Truman to Nixon approved it.

Additional control or regulatory bodies, ostensibly created to effect adequate supervision over the CIA, included the President's Foreign Intelligence Advisory Board, a group of eleven presidential appointees. This organization was brought into existence by

President Dwight Eisenhower in 1956, with the hope in mind that eleven citizens selected from non-government circles might be dispassionately uninvolved and thus capable of critical judgments.

There was nothing wrong with the idea except that since the United States government, particularly the Pentagon, was the single largest supporter of the United States economy, it was next to impossible to select even eleven United States citizens who were not either directly or indirectly beneficiaries of some federally funded project.

The result was that the President's Foreign Intelligence Advisory Board was anything but dispassionate or critical. It did not help much, either, that Dwight Eisenhower, who had himself spent his entire lifespan as a federally funded career soldier, appointed other old soldiers to the board.

The CIA did not have to penetrate this group, nor did it have to strive for influence with the one organization of government which, theoretically at least, had both the incentive and the mandated power to control it—the Office of Management and Budget.

The OMB had responsibility for monitoring departmental spending. It had authority to order the suspension of programmes which were excessively expensive, or which were not likely to meet priority requirements. It was supported by the president and had a record going back to earlier days when it was known as the Bureau of the Budget, for being flintily obdurate.

It even had a separate bureau, called the International Affairs Division, whose duty was to carefully scrutinize all Intelligence budgets and expenditures.

The reason the agency did not have to strive for influence over the OMB was that, in 1962, a man named Robert Amory Jr became chief of the OMB's International Affairs Division. Amory was a former CIA Deputy Director of Intelligence, one-time Presidential Intelligence Adviser, and a long-time CIA official whose service went back to the Dulles years.

Also, one of the OMB's civilian examiners was recruited by the CIA, then put to work collaborating with his successor—who also was a former CIA employee. This time the penetration had to be deep, and obviously, it was.

The list of control organizations was by no means small. Every United States President from Dwight Eisenhower to Gerald Ford, has been troubled by the need to find an answer to the problem of the monolithic United States Intelligence apparatus. None has succeeded, and in fact the proliferation of control groups, including those sponsored by the Congress, must total well into the hundreds without evidence appearing, anywhere in the White House, the Congress, Academy, or the strident news media, which would support a contention that the answer does not lie in control at all, it lies in the development of a United States political philosophy which would not alienate foreigners, but which would inspire both foreigners *and* Americans.

Consistently to seek controls is equivalent to admitting that there is no better, third way of resolving humankind's snowballing problems than by the identical policies, and political philosophies, which inspired Bismarck, Napoleon, and Adolf Hitler, but there surely must be.

A State Department incapable of shedding the Dulles chrysalis a quarter century after it became empty of meaning, and an executive branch unwilling to seek solutions instead of controls, deserves exactly what it owns, an intelligence community which numbers in excess of one million people, and which consumes the second largest percentage of the United States tax dollar, and obtains that kind of wealth and power largely through subterfuge.

There will always be an Intelligence bureaucracy, and until *détente* becomes something different from what it presently is, a deliberate variety of consummate deceit, there will also continue to be an immense KGB and a monolithic CIA.

Control is no answer, but if it were, if someone could devise a means for de-fanging the Central Intelligence Agency, then all that would be accomplished would be the elimination of *our* monolith, leaving us at the untender mercy of *their* monolith, and clearly, that kind of an answer is no answer at all.

Still, each spring political figures come forth as regularly as the crocuses, denouncing the clandestine mentality, which they invariably equate with the CIA, expounding on the evils and immorality (or amorality) of espionage, subversion, international meddling, then hurry home to their constituencies to be re-elected, heroes of the New Morality, champions of beleaguered taxpayers against the stunningly profligate Central Intelligence Agency, and only one accomplishment has actually been achieved: the CIA has been vilified—again.

It does not fall. It does not even falter, because every knowledgeable, rationally realistic taxpayer, *and* his political representatives, are quite aware that, staggeringly expensive and often inept though the CIA may be, in the real world, no one has yet come forth with an acceptable alternative.

There is something else most taxpayers do not appear to realize. Fond though everyone is of denouncing the CIA, and blaming it for everything from invidious acne to incipient pregnancy, it is *not* the most skilled, nor even at its maximum-allowable personnel status, the largest United States Intelligence organization. That distinction belongs to the far less advertised, ultra secret, National Security Agency, which was originally organized in 1952 to be an Intelligence-accumulating adjunct of the Department of Defence.

NSA subsequently established itself independently, and at the present time has a work-force of 25,000 people, a budget in excess of a billion and a half dollars annually, and has direct affiliations with the three major United States armed forces, Army, Navy, and Air Force, in over two hundred Intelligence posts throughout the world.

NSA headquarters, at Fort Meade, Maryland, has undoubtedly the most prodigious collection of intercepted messages in the world. NSA is an eavesdropping organization on a scale, and in a manner, no writer of espionage fiction could imagine. It has cryptological equipment capable of decoding nearly every secret code ever devised, and for those codes its cryptologists have been unable to decipher—yet—it has enormous vault facilities where these messages are kept while some of the most ingenious scientists in the world work at the development of new machines which will ultimately be able to decipher the indecipherable messages.

NSA maintains a constant aerial and satellite surveillance of every nation on earth. It makes no distinction between friends of the United States or possible foes in its round-the-clock monitoring. Its ability to decipher Communist Chinese diplomatic and Intelligence codes gave NSA a distinct intelligence advantage over every other Intelligence organization, including the Central Intelligence Agency.

The spy-vessel, USS *Pueblo*, captured by North Korea in 1968, was an NSA ship. The spy-ship shelled by the Israelis in 1967, the *Liberty*, was another NSA vessel. NSA spy-aircraft have rather consistently produced espionage results better than those of any other Western Intelligence agency including the Central Intelligence Agency.

Finally the National Security Agency, not the CIA, owns the largest and most sophisticated computer bank in the world, and until two of its younger members, Bernon Mitchell and William Martin, defected to the USSR in 1960 and subsequently made candid disclosures about the NSA, neither the Soviets nor most Westerners, including Americans, knew that the National Security Agency, not the Central Intelligence Agency, was the West's largest Intelligence organization.

The reason the NSA has managed to avoid the variety of publicity which has plagued the CIA, has been because the National Security Agency is exclusively an eavesdropping facility; it employs few secret agents and indulges in no covert, clandestine, or paramilitary activity. It is entirely an ultra-secret electronics spying and listening-decoding organization.

13

'The Associates'

Intelligence personnel—particularly spies—inhabit a separate environment, and like many dedicated professionals have more in common with those against whom they compete than they have in common with others.

During World War II an outstanding French tank officer, sentenced to death when captured by the Germans, was saved from execution by an invalided former German tank officer at the death-camp reception centre, where the German read the Frenchman's war-record. They shared something other Germans or Frenchmen did not share. Generally, this same kind of affinity has applied in the world of espionage, even though similar gallantry is rare.

Intelligence people are 'associates'. They share anxieties, perils, the identical sensations over triumphs and failures, and they can more readily appreciate whatever befalls another spy, ally or enemy than an ordinary citizen can.

They understand every nuance, every rule and every risk of their trade. As individuals, professional spies are better actors than motion picture luminaries, better impersonators than famous mimics, and better perceptionists and sensitives than most psychic mediums. Finally, after years at their trade they become better imitation schizoids—without ever actually being schizophrenics because they cannot afford the luxury of genuine schizophrenia.

Espionage is certainly not a game and yet its rules are basically the same as the rules of competitive sports. Enemy networks strive endlessly to prevent one another from acquiring information, while simultaneously seeking to gain as much information as they can from their opposition. Every Intelligence precaution is a challenge to the 'other side'. Orthodox behaviour and common law are invoked when needed, and completely ignored otherwise. Espionage and counter-espionage, two sides of the same coin, require great concentration, dedication, and steel nerves. They also require extraordinary sensitivity—almost genuine perspicacity—and unalterable persistence. The greatest secret agents have been those who have led successful dual lives sometimes for ten or twenty years, occasionally for entire lifetimes, in order to be 'in place'—active and totally unsuspected—for perhaps no more than four or five times in all that period.

The German spy posing as a watchmaker who made possible the fatal U-boat attack upon Britain's great warship *Ark Royal* during the Second World War, had been 'in place' for almost fifteen years; had, in fact become a British citizen well before the war broke out.

It has historically been this type of absolute and unquestioning dedication which has produced some of the most spectacular espionage and counter-espionage successes.

Most European nations, with centuries of expertise derived from trial and error, have perfected the Intelligence function. Germany, past-master of the science, made an uncommon error in World War II when its leadership became so obsessed with Intelligence that it had Intelligence agencies falling over one another. Like the United States thirty years later, the emphasis was on the quantity rather than the quality of Intelligence.

The French were better, at least during the war when they were an occupied sovereignty, but subsequently their Intelligence network was considered by most other professionals to be no better than a kind of Mafia-type organization, involved in bribery, political blackmail, and extortion.

The British, primarily the English, while technically not Europeans were nonetheless the most accomplished spies and counterspies of Europe. One of their great spymasters was the first Queen Elizabeth's 'Moor', Sir Francis Walsingham, whose exploits remain to this day, roughly four hundred years later, an epitome of what successful espionage is all about. From Walsingham to the present chief of Britain's MI6 British Intelligence successes have been steady and often spectacular. If the British apparatus had a weakness it had to lie in the area of personnel screening; defectors from sensitive positions have been a cause of considerable aggravation, over the past generation in particular. MI6 shares this misfortune with most other Intelligence organizations, of course, including

American reconnaissance photograph of missile launch site, San Diego de los Baños, Cuba, October 1962

Nuclear warhead storage bunker under construction in San Cristobal, Cuba (*and below*) Soviet missiles at Casilda Port, Cuba

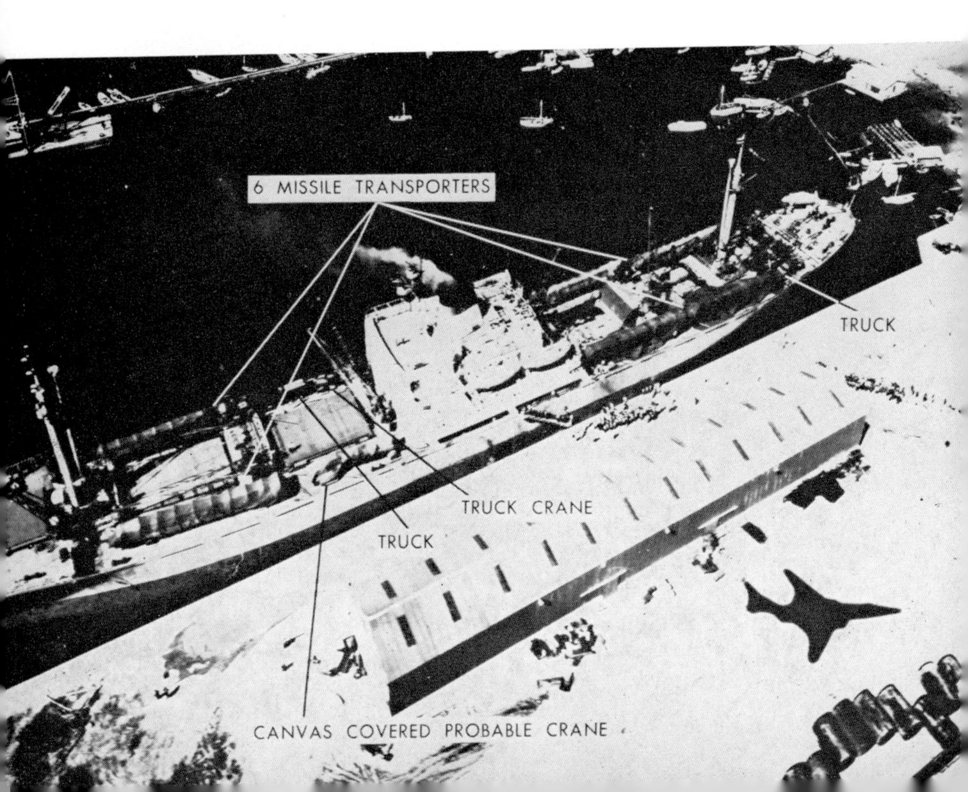

the CIA and the KGB, but that fact hardly minimizes the embarrassment.

Britain's MI6, a general equivalent to the CIA, at least to the extent that MI6 is concerned with foreign Intelligence, (as opposed to MI5, which, like the FBI handles internal security) has several distinct advantages over United States Intelligence agencies. Foremost is Britain's Official Secrets Act which provides penalties for the disclosure of specific restricted and classified information. Prosecution under this act can be undertaken without public disclosure of the classified material itself. Through the 'D Notice' system, British publishers are invited voluntarily to abstain from making public anything which would compromise military secrets, and since the Official Secrets Act is entirely enforceable, few deliberate violations occur.

Americans, most particularly those concerned with selling newspapers, denounce any such act for the United States on the grounds that it violates the First Amendment to the Constitution —the guarantee of free speech. They also denounce it as a Gestapo-type procedure of dictatorial oppression, and yet Britain, which has had its Official Secrets Act since 1911, almost sixty-five years, and which is a nation noted for protecting individual freedom, has benefited rather than suffered from this sensible and practical article of legislation.

Another advantage MI6 enjoys, is a very professional attitude toward espionage of quiet anonymity, which seems to be based upon Thomas Carlyle's observation that 'He who has a secret should not only hide it, but hide that he has it to hide'.

MI6, operating under a misnomer to start with, since 'MI' signifies 'military Intelligence' and MI6 is not a military organization, functions in a false vacuum. It is never officially acknowledged to exist, and its director is never officially—and rarely unofficially—referred to by name. He is mentioned, when at all, as 'M' or 'C', or simply as the 'Director General'.

Nevertheless, every active Intelligence organization not only knows of MI6, but who its current director is, (Sir John Ogilvy Rennie, in 1973) and by name and speciality who most of its agents are.

As for penetration, MI6 spies operate worldwide, with less urgency than a quarter century ago, and earlier, but they are active on four continents. The association between MI6 and the

CIA has been of long standing.

MI6 agents have operated in the United States for two hundred years. During two awkward interludes—1776–1781, and 1812–1814—they were enemy agents. (During the 1812–1814 awkwardness the British burned the United States Executive Mansion. When it was restored, painted completely white, it acquired its popular name : the White House.)

Recently, MI6 agents have been especially interested in Irish-Americans, particularly those involved with secretly supplying arms to Northern Ireland, and those making pro-Irish, anti-British broadcasts, or appearing at IRA fund-raising events as speakers or contributors.

This penetration was sanctioned by former US President Nixon, and co-operation between a generally friendly CIA and Britain's MI6 has occasioned a considerable exchange of Intelligence information.

Over the years, since World War II, CIA and MI6 have largely been very similar. It was MI6 which first recruited Colonel Oleg Penkovskiy, senior Soviet military officer, Russian hero of World War II, graduate of the Soviet Staff college and missile academy, (who was sentenced to death and shot in Moscow in early 1963). MI6 eventually delivered Penkovskiy to the CIA, which he served as an 'in place' spy until he was 'uncovered', tried and executed.

Throughout the Penkovskiy affair the CIA and MI6 performed flawlessly together. Association among Intelligence organizations is not actually uncommon. A fair example would be the publication by the United States publishing house of Little, Brown and Company of Boston, Massachusetts (34 Beacon Street), of the memoirs of former Soviet Premier Nikita Khrushchev.

The Khrushchev memoirs, (entitled *Khrushchev Remembers*) which came directly to their publisher through Soviet channels, were studied by all United States Intelligence officials. They were, in fact, proof-read, and a set of galley proofs were returned to Moscow by United States Intelligence, for final approval, and were then returned, by Soviet Intelligence, suitable for publication.

The purpose, obviously, was to present Western readers with a dose of high-level Soviet propaganda. On the United States side, the advantage of co-operation was political—it would strengthen the United States policy of *détente* and co-operation. From the Intelligence standpoint it demonstrated the fact of secret co-operation, which had occurred before between the CIA and the KGB, who have otherwise been traditional and hostile enemies for a generation.

Occasionally, the secret co-operation goes deeper and becomes more complex. For example, when MI6 and its internal security corollary MI5 uncovered a massive Soviet espionage network active in Britain in 1971, it passed along to the United States the warning that, according to its KGB informant, the same in-depth penetration was then taking place in the United States.

The KGB defector who alerted the British was seeking asylum in Britain, and brought with him from the Soviet Embassy a voluminous exposé of the entire Soviet espionage network in Britain.

The British reaction was predictable; after a thorough investigation, ninety Russians were ordered to leave Britain, and the visas of an additional fifteen Soviet citizens were withdrawn.

There was nothing in the classified information supplied by the Russian defector to suggest the same kind of massive penetration was taking place in the United States, but the defector assured the British that in fact it was, and on the strength of this the United States government was warned.

This was not a CIA area. United States internal security was the responsibility of the Federal Bureau of Investigation. The FBI, far from being alarmed, was almost sanguine. It had over five hundred Soviet citizens in the United States under surveillance. They were all spies and most of them were masquerading as either trade officials, diplomats or newsmen. It had dossiers on Russians who had engaged in espionage, who had incited civil disturbances within the United States, who had tried to recruit Americans for Soviet espionage, and who had visited colleges across the country developing contacts among student radicals.

None of these people were expelled from the country. When the FBI sought their expulsion the State Department demurred on the grounds that any mass action like the one employed by the British would damage the prospects of *détente*. The best the FBI could accomplish was to maintain a tightened surveillance.

Out of this bizarre affair arose a situation where associated Intelligence organizations, MI6 and the FBI (with the CIA a silent partner), co-operated in the development of adequate evidence to result in the expulsion of hundreds of KGB spies from the United States, and the Russians were protected by the United States government.

One of these Soviet spies, Galina Utekhina, a cultural attaché at the Soviet Embassy in Washington, cultivated United States politicians and upper-level government employees. She was a very attractive and persuasive KGB agent. Another was Oleg Kalugin —also known as Victor Kraknikovich—who recruited a Greek-born American as a Soviet spy. The recruit went to the FBI and was counter-recruited, and through him the identity and whereabouts of other Soviet agents was learned—without any of them, including Oleg Kalugin, being expelled.

Co-operation between foreign governments at the diplomatic level is certainly common enough, even between ideological hostile governments, but below that level, at the Intelligence level, co-operation between competing networks as a rule cannot rely on the kind of assinine delusion demonstrated by the State Department as in the foregoing affair. The closest the Soviets have come actually to protecting United States spies has been in the case of exchanges. Francis Gary Powers, the U-2 spyplane pilot shot down, presumably over Soviet territory in early 1962, was offered to the United States in exchange for KGB agent Rudolf Abel. The following year, in the early summer of 1963, the Soviets proposed a trade with the British. They offered MI6 agent Greville Wynn, Oleg Penkovskiy's contact, for seven Soviet agents, all minor ones excepting Gordon Lonsdale, who, unlike the others, was a Soviet citizen, and who was also a skilled and dedicated agent. The trade was made, marking another instance in which the association of Intelligence agencies achieved success.

There have also been instances when enemy networks have collaborated to conceal facts, and to hide private schemes from the public of their respective countries, as though Intelligence organizations existed in a separate jungle from those whose taxes supported them.

The Germans of both camps, East and West, have occasionally managed an association. Germany was, throughout the 1950s and 1960s, the espionage capital of the West. The Central Intelligence Agency maintained a formidable presence there. It funded political parties, student groups, labour organizations, even hotels and restaurants. Its listening posts in the German Federal

Republic (West Germany) were very sophisticated and also very productive.

During the 'Cold War' CIA activity in West Germany increased yearly, and afterwards, by the year 1968, the CIA's West German installation was the largest, outside the United States, of any CIA station. There were a number of reasons. Aside from its adjacency to Communist East Germany, which provided the CIA with a window towards a Soviet satellite, West Germany was centrally located to conduct espionage activities in every direction. It was also centrally located for the reception of defectors, from every direction, and until the erection of the Berlin Wall in 1961 an estimated four million East Germans, alone, crossed out of the Communist east zone. These people were an invaluable source of information. Also, among that great horde came Communist spies from Poland, East Germany, Czechoslovakia, every Iron Curtain country, and such non-Communist nations as Austria, Italy, the Netherlands, and France.

The espionage opportunities, too, were extensive. CIA personnel could remain safely in West Germany, then disappear into the Soviet satellite adjacencies with relative ease, while counter-Intelligence people, responsible for the protection of CIA and allied espionage activities within the Federal Republic, had constantly to devise new exposure techniques, the result of enemy attempts at penetration.

West Germany, beginning with the reconstruction and rehabilitation period subsequent to World War II and up to the present time, has probably been the most spied *upon* and spied *from* country in recent history.

Here, the CIA acquired some of its most valuable Communist-bloc defectors. People whose association with Intelligence work in several satellite nations as well as the Soviet Union has enabled the agency to remain current on significant changes behind the Iron Curtain, and one fact stands out: most defectors from Soviet domination fade, or at least attempt to fade, into anonymous obscurity once they reach the West—but not Intelligence people. Invariably, they seek out other Intelligence people. They are 'the associates'. They are never soldiers, technicians, agrarianists, instructors, whatever their original background or training qualified them for, they are Intelligence people, and they seek out their own kind, even though that may lead them to a possible enemy.

These people can collaborate, even while they are ideological enemies, more successfully than can alien doctors, storekeepers, van drivers or farmers. They do not generally talk to the police to whom many turn themselves in as defectors. They wait until they are in the custody of other Intelligence people to speak candidly. When they seek asylum they do so as former Intelligence people, whether they were actually part of an espionage or counter-espionage apparatus, or whether they were simply cryptologists, analysts, interpreters or clerks.

They rarely make any attempt to conceal a former Intelligence connection. The nature of the work and the training marks them, and even those who do not or who cannot return to the Intelligence vocation, nevertheless retain all the characteristics on into the future.

It may be, as has been said many times, that only a certain kind of person can succeed at espionage, and in sequence, it may then also be true that this special variety of person has already been marked for the Intelligence speciality long before he becomes involved with it, in which case he would retain the characteristics of an 'associate' whether he ever became espionage-oriented or not.

Whether this is applicable, or whether the work, the training, the unique environment of espionage, unlike any other environment, is responsible, one thing is amply clear, the affinity exists; active, inactive, retired or 'burned out', professional Intelligence people are all associated regardless of what—or which—system they serve or have served.

14

A Quadrangle and Quicksand

Going back approximately thirty years to 1947 when a victorious free world was in as much disarray as a result of victory as the Fascist world was as a result of defeat, it was possible to locate only two systems capable of an adequate recovery out of the half dozen systems which had existed at the beginning of the Second World War, and both of these systems were notably flawed. The Communists had organizations and zealotry, plus stultification, on their side. The Freedomists had wealth, resources, and everlasting internal dissension on their side.

The struggle between the two systems which culminated in the Cold War and its murky conclusion left Communism's lean cadres gnawing at the exposed flanks of the rehabilitated nations, and definitely in control of the historic Balkan buffer lying between the Adriatic and the Black Sea, leaving two particular areas, West Germany and the Ionian-Aegean quadrangle, temptingly vulnerable.

Free Germany, disarmed, dismembered, and with Red Poland separating it from its old antagonist Russia, was not a threat.

Neither was the Ionian-Aegean quadrangle a threat actually, but being an appendage to the Soviet Balkans, and certainly within the Soviet shadow while physically apart from Free Europe, it was a temptation and it *was* vulnerable. War had ravished Greece, allied with the victors, and the same conflict had impoverished Turkey, whose ambivalence had been a source of annoyance to both sides during the war. Also, Turkey more than Greece, was an old foe, and finally Soviet power extending to the quadrangle and beyond, would make the warm Mediterranean a Soviet lake.

However, the USSR had also been impoverished by the war. It could not mount a costly effort, nor could it openly invade Greece and Turkey. It did not already have armed force in those lands, as had been the case throughout the Balkans, therefore the remaining alternative was to fund and encourage the native Communist movements, and this course was embarked upon. However, as in Korea and Berlin, the United States hardened its position. Financial, as well as military and technical aid were sent to the quadrangle, and by the 1950s both Greece and Turkey had become Western outposts.

But keeping the Communists out, desirable though it may have been, was only one aspect of a situation rooted in an ancient past. This was precisely the kind of a problem Henry Kissinger was never able competently to understand; his dollar-diplomacy approach, here, as in the Middle East and south-east Asia was unable to resolve differences which money has never really been able to correct. The constituents of the quadrangle, Greece and Turkey, were not friends. To arm and supply both was the equivalent to a guarantee that as soon as the shadow of the Red Star waned these ancient antagonists would return, well fed and well armed, to their historic antagonism.

Turkey became a bastion for the free world's North Atlantic Treaty Organization. United States wealth helped create a formidable Turkish armed service. Greece also became a pro-Western arsenal. Free-world aid more than augmented the living—and fighting—standards of these two countries, it also injected fresh impetus into ancient ambitions, and what Dr Kissinger never understood, that history, too, is a weapon, ultimately resurrected the old antagonisms, but now with more risk for everyone, and those lean cadremen of the Soviet system, sensing the vacuum created by indecision and worry in Washington and by the uneasy posturing of the quadrangle's old Aegean rivals, began to exacerbate the situation.

Almost thirty years had passed since the initial peril had existed; a long enough time for a better solution than dollar diplomacy to have been devised. No better solution *had* been devised, and when friction developed, but before trouble came, the United States response was CIA-oriented.

As a matter of fact the American Intelligence apparatus had long been established in both Greece and Turkey. Officials of both countries had been accepting CIA support for years, with the difference that in Turkey the approach to aid of all kinds, had been realistically tough, but acceptance of largesse did not go quite as far as exchanging total confidences. The Turks had never surrendered their independence, and despite all that was given by the Turks in the way of assurances, the Americans had reason to be wary after being caught unprepared by the generals' revolt of 1960.

Greece had always been more philosophical about United States aid. CIA money had bought some of Greece's ablest parliamentarians. It supported the Greek military junta which overthrew Archbishop Makarios on Cyprus. It funded 'Little Nikos' Sampson, Makarios's Cypriot competitor, a man whose speciality was shooting people in the back. (He boasted of having slain twenty-five British soldiers in this fashion.) Makarios, himself, accepted CIA money. He got it by blackmail. One of Greece's most respected publishers, Savyas Konstantopoulos, who influenced public opinion through his *Athens Free Press*, was on the CIA payroll for many years. So was Brigadier General Dimitrios Ioannidis, for a while the uncontested ruler of Greece.

A Greek-born CIA agent named Peter Koromilas was General Ioannidis's confidant and adviser. It was this agent who reported to CIA headquarters, weeks in advance of the junta's overthrow of Makarios on Cyprus, that this was Ioannidis's intention.

The CIA's best effort at stopping the *coup* were not very good, and in the behind-the-scenes manipulating which followed the *coup* some power—thought to have been the USSR—incited a fresh palace revolution and the overthrow of Makarios at that particular time brought about a Turkish invasion of Cyprus at a time when only Greek-Cypriot's were adequately unified to resist. Greece, itself, was torn by centrist, rightist, and leftist factionalism.

Turkey had little trouble in overrunning the areas of Cyprus it invaded, while in Athens the Ioannidis junta was ousted, the General, who actually was only the chief of military police, and his figurehead President, Phaidon Gizikis, yielding to pressures exerted against them by Greek army, navy, and air force leadership.

The result was not especially unpleasant in Greece, but on the island of Cyprus it was disastrous. For several days after the fall of Dimitrios Ioannnidis Greece was without any leadership. A former premier who was residing in Paris, Constantine Karamanlis, was contacted and most urgently requested to return to Athens to form a new government, and although he eventually accepted the offer and returned, meanwhile, on Cyprus the embattled Greek Cypriots, while handily outnumbering Turkish Cypriots, were no match for a mainland Turkish army.

Atrocities were committed. Greeks died by the hundreds and from Greece itself no aid arrived. There was no leadership. Greeks in Athens, inflamed and frustrated at the spectacle of their countrymen being butchered on Cyprus, seeking a cause—and of course a scapegoat—resurrected an old allegation, one which Greeks had been garrulously employing for twenty years: CIA involvement in Greek politics had brought about the current mess, and in fact had been responsible for the establishment of the last two military juntas, that of George Papadopoulos, which was inaugurated in the spring of 1967, and which lasted until the fall of Papadopoulos in 1972, and his replacement with another junta, this one controlled by Ioannidis, which in turn yielded to Constantine Karamanlis in 1974 as a result of the Cyprus *débâcle*.

Anti-Americanism was inevitable and in due course it came in the form of mass demonstrations, looting, burning, and finally, in mid-August of 1974, at Nicosia on the Island of Cyprus, the United States Ambassador, Rodger P. Davies, was deliberately killed in a carefully planned and expertly co-ordinated assassination.

This did not mark an end to either the Cyprus fighting or the outbursts of anti-Americanism in Greece. If anything, it appeared to crystallize Greek sentiment. Demands were made that the United States get out of Greece, which was not only a pivotal NATO stronghold but which was also honeycombed with United States naval, air force, military, and CIA installations.

The CIA began moving some of its more sensitive operations out. By the time the Karamanlis government responded to Greek anger the agency had re-established many of its former Greek functions elsewhere, most notably in Iran, but the implications went considerably deeper. For one thing, the outraged Greeks threatened to abandon the North Atlantic Treaty Organization. For another, Greek leftists, moving swiftly into the vacuum, encouraged Greek resentment, and more than doubled their Greek membership. Finally, the CIA involvement was vituperatively denounced, and while a lot of the allegations were not true, enough of them *were* true to antagonize uninvolved, worldwide onlookers.

The results are far from finished in 1975. It could be expected that Greek indignation would demand a United States withdrawal from some Greek bases, that CIA interference in Greece's internal affairs cease, and it could also be expected that the exultant Soviets would manoeuvre their cadremen into the vacuum created by this falling-out of allies.

Aside from the tempestuous furore, and behind all the denials, allegations, accusations and bombast, all the furious exchanges on both sides, exacerbated of course by the Communists, lies a middle-ground of fact: what, exactly, was the extent of the Central Intelligence Agency's involvement?

To find the initial answer go back a number of years to the establishment of the United States role in Greece, beginning with the ousting of an earlier, more liberal régime, and the investiture of the Papadopoulos dictatorship in April of 1967.

United States interests being synonymous with those of the North Atlantic Treaty Organization, and United States financial aid to NATO being considerable, it was essential in the view of United States planners that two factors should obtain. One was that Greece agree to permit United States forces to use Greece as a Mediterranean base. This was done. The second requirement was that the Greek government be stable. Earlier governments, including that of General John Metaxas, which preceded the Papadopoulos dictatorship, lasted four and a half years. Other Greek governments did not even last that long.

It would have been useless to create the kind of Greek bastion United States and NATO leaders envisaged, and to spend the hundreds of millions of dollars this would require, if, upon completion or even before, an unfriendly régime came to power. The United States government supported George Papadopoulos. It did this with bribery, military aid and economic assistance. It had the Central Intelligence Agency to use as a funnel for a cash-flow, but also the CIA functioned in Greece as it had elsewhere; in the capacity of an overseer, not always a discreet one, but usually as an efficient one.

The charge was made often that the United States—meaning of course the CIA—supported a dictatorship. This was true. It was also true that a dictatorship in the Balkans, in the areas across the Mediterranean from Greece, in Africa, or on around the far coastline, in Syria, Jordan, Saudi Arabia and elsewhere, was the norm. Democracies and Republics, even constitutional monarchies, were not common in that part of the world. Nor has it been very abundantly demonstrated that even in Greece, the so-called cradle of democracy, the elective process endures for long. The current Premier, Constantine Karamanlis, judging by past experience, will last four to five years and no longer.

There has never been any genuinely valid reason for assuming that all dictatorships are bad—or that all democratic processes are good. The Central Intelligence Agency's concern in Greece, as elsewhere, was stability. That the CIA has undeniably supported many dictatorships is based upon a very simple fact of international political life : in this world there are many more dictatorships than there are republics.

The Greeks were not especially averse to the Papadopoulos régime. They enjoyed intellectual freedom, and for the seven years it endured they had unprecedented prosperity. The annual national income for Greece's nine million people rose under Papadopoulos from $816 to $1,225, business throve, industrial growth and modernization flourished.

There were also some unpleasant statistics, such as 7,000 arrests in the early stages of the dictatorship, subsequently pared down in the last year before Papadopoulos's fall to only about 350. Also, dissident generals were removed from the path of temptation, and until the student revolt of 1973 martial law was very minimal, but the armed forces clearly ran the nation, a fact Britons, Americans and others would not especially approve of, but then Greece was not the United States nor Britain.

The CIA's penetration was deep. The agency owned Greek politicians by the score, and newsmen by the dozens. It abetted Papadopoulos's moves to confirm himself in power. Its tentacles reached into every phase of Greek life; they had to. For centuries Greece had been a boiling political cauldron; the risk of losing that huge NATO investment as well as the strategic importance of Greece's Mediterranean position, demanded nothing less.

But the CIA *was* 'in place', it *did* interfere in the internal affairs of Greece. What it did *not* do, although it was clamorously accused of it, was create the climate for Dimitrios Ioannidis to overthrow George Papadopoulos. On the face of it, this would make no sense at all. Papadopoulos's shortcomings were many, but as an alternative, Ioannidis, described by United States Ambassador to Greece, Henry Tasca, as an incredibly 'uninformed [and] incompetent . . .' individual, was far worse, and he proved it by engineering the plot to depose Archbishop Makarios in Cyprus at the precise moment when Greek-Turkish friction in Cyprus, as well as unrest in Greece, was at a dangerous peak. The United States position in Greece had never been better than it was under George Papadopoulos. It was never worse than under Ioannidis.

The CIA knew, long before the *coup*, exactly the kind of man Dimitrios Ioannidis was. It would not have chosen him as a replacement for Papadopoulos. Why then, did not the CIA stop Ioannidis? It tried. Both Peter Koromalis, the CIA representative who was Ioannidis's confidant, and Ambassador Tasca did their utmost to dissuade Ioannidis from moving against Archbishop Makarios. Ioannidis, a capable-enough in-fighter, with control of Greece's 20,000-man military police apparatus, saw his triumph over Papadopoulos as proof that he was anyone's equal, and he refused to be dissuaded with the sanguinary results which ensued.

In sum and in total, the CIA involvement in Greece was no less than the British MI6 had experienced years earlier, and before the British, other Intelligence organizations had also experienced.

Greece was a political quagmire; it had been nothing better for centuries. Strategically, the fortunes of an always-changing international spectrum had made Greece important again by coming full circle from the days when it was a city-state called Athens, and its neighbours were called Macedonia, Epirus, Achaia, Psidia, Lycia, and Cilicia, but since those days to 1975, it had not changed in its garrulousness, its unpredictability, its changing moods, its Greek temperament.

Under Constantine Karamanlis it would change again and beyond Karamanlis it would change still again. The Central Intelligence Agency, like Xerxes, was unable to prevail, but unlike Xerxes, the CIA did not have a Themistocles in opposition to it, but there was the same, enduring, mercurial Greek temperament, and even Themistocles had never found a way to cope fully with that.

15

How to Lose While Winning

Simple answers to the major questions in either the espionage or political spheres are non-existent. As an example, any assessments of the Cyprus affair must, therefore, reach back well before the 1974–75 difficulties in order to achieve a coherent sequence. They must, in fact, go back even prior to Great Britain's concessions at the 1959 Treaty of London conference which smoothed the way for the establishment of an independent Cyprus.

They must fully recognize that the miscegenated population of Cyprus is eighty per cent Greek, or at least Greek-speaking, as well as upholding the traditions and customs of Greece.

They must further recognize that the majority population of Cyprus is antagonistic to Turkey, while the Island of Cyprus is just off-shore from Turkey. The closeness of all those hostile Greeks, plus the nightmare possibility of the island being used as a staging area by an aggressor quite understandably has kept the Turks emotionally as well as defensively concerned for generations.

When the United States stabilized Greek and Turkish economics, then underwrote the modernization of Greek and Turkish armed services, it did those things in order to protect a NATO flank. It did *not* do these things in order to strengthen either antagonist against the other but regardless of good intentions the ancient antagonisms *were* strengthened. To repeat: history too is a weapon. Those who would overlook or ignore this are the people George Santayana probably had in mind in his dictum about history repeating itself.

The solution? There probably is none. There certainly is no simple answer, and even the currently popular idea of a cantonment accord, which is not at all new, does not resolve the basic dilemma, the ancient antagonism. It particularly does little towards promoting good-will and trust after the spectacularly successful 1974 Turkish invasion, which, in the words of a British observer, left the cities, ports and industries in Turkish control, while the Greeks controlled the grapes.

For the Central Intelligence Agency historic Cyprus has been an outsize headache. Since earliest times it has been nothing better than that to innumerable foreigners, and especially to its most recent governors, the British. For a thousand years smouldering factionalism has existed. The problems of Cyprus have never, but especially in recent times, lent themselves to any kind of ready solutions, and while periods of economic depression have in the past dampened the hostility of the antagonists because there was no money available for anything but sporadic and inconclusive sniping, stabilizing the Greek and Turkish economics, arming and modernizing Greek and Turkish defence forces, most certainly and inevitably breathed new life into the ancient hostility.

What, it has been asked, were the alternatives, and the answer, based upon the North Atlantic Treaty Organization's requirements, is clearly evident: abandon the quadrangle as an outpost of the Free World, or make it a bastion—headaches and all.

NATO adopted the latter course, and as a matter of fact was admirably successful at maintaining a peaceful balance for many years, and meanwhile the Communists, well aware of the weakness in this scheme—the age-old Greek-Turkish antipathy—employed their Intelligence contacts in the quadrangle to upset the uneasy balance.

Four years prior to the most recent (1974–75) violence, in the early part of 1970, the Cypriot Communist Party (CCP) very nearly evoked the same kind of an uprising they more successfully encouraged in 1974. They accomplished this by warning the Soviet Embassy at Nicosia that Greek army officers were plotting to overthrow the island's bipartisan government.

The Central Intelligence Agency, active on the island, knew only that the historic Greek-Turkish antagonism flourished. It had no information about any impending *coup* for a very good reason: there was no such plot.

There was *talk* of an overthrow, and the protagonists of *enosis* (union with Greece) were serious, but that was hardly novel. Scarcely a year had passed since 1959 when one side or the other had not advocated total partisanship, either Greek or Turkish, or had not accused the other side of plotting to accomplish it.

The Soviets at Nicosia undertook a quiet investigation while simultaneously informing Moscow of the CCP warning. Subsequently, when the Nicosia investigation turned up no corroboration of the CCP warning, a report to this effect was forwarded to Moscow.

Now, the Soviet KGB Disinformation Centre (Department D, first Directorate) immediately moved into the vacuum. The Soviet Ambassador to Turkey, Vasili F. Grubyakov, formerly a high KGB official, was instructed to go at once to the Turkish Foreign Office in Ankara and inform the leadership privately there that the USSR had uncovered a CIA plot to overthrow the government of Cyprus, and to install an all-Greek junta antagonistic to Turkey. The alleged purpose of this scheme, according to the Soviets, was to claim Cyprus for Greece and turn it into a vast NATO base which could be used to coerce Turkey into complying with whatever additional schemes the CIA might be considering.

The secret meeting at which this 'plot' was revealed to the Turkish Foreign Minister by Ambassador Grubyakov occurred late at night in March of 1970. The following morning the Turkish government announced its discovery of the 'plot'.

Meanwhile the Soviet Ambassador instructed a number of Bulgarian diplomats stationed in Ankara to announce additional confirmation of the scheme, and Soviet Intelligence officials delivered KGB news releases to the Turkish press. The results were predictable. Government officials in Ankara, news services, officials of the armed services and common citizens, were outraged.

The CIA, with considerable experience in the field of 'black propaganda'—or 'disinformation'—had no difficulty in correctly analysing the situation. The Turks were informed but the KGB had done its job well. Knowledgeable Turks, reluctant in the face of a national furore to oppose it, or to speak favourably of the CIA or the USA, said nothing. They could not have reversed, nor even very effectively have ameliorated the storm of anti-Americanism in any case, and an attempt to do either would certainly have been politically fatal.

At the peak of the tumult demands were made for Turkish military action against the Greeks of Cyprus.

For the Central Intelligence Agency, an inauguration of counter-measures was the natural response, but in the realm of

Commander Anthony Courtney whose career was damaged by an indiscretion

Greville Wynne, the British businessman charged by the Russians with espionage, photographed during his trial

Intelligence, as in most other endeavours, there is no substitute for first-strike initiative.

What ultimately defused the situation was the fact that there had never been any such plot, and Turkish agents on Cyprus turned up no evidence that such a plot had existed. But the historically susceptible antagonism had been exploited, and even those who subsequently became convinced the entire affair had been contrived, could not readily forget the *possibility*, at a future time, of the same scheme or a similar one evolving.

Soviet culpability was never the issue. In fact the Soviet scheme had been so successful that even when it was eventually disclosed as being completely false, Soviet prestige, while it suffered to some degree, paid a very small price for the discovery that in the future a similar plan, more sophisticated and less spontaneous, would succeed, and of course it *did* succeed in 1974 when Turkey invaded Cyprus, killed hundreds of Greek Cypriots, and assumed military domination of the island. It also succeeded in driving a solid wedge between the Turks, the leaderless Greeks and their sponsors, NATO and the USA, which was the Soviet purpose.

The CIA, which was a defensive implement of both NATO and the USA, had over the decades disrupted many plots in the quadrangle, not all of them, in fact not even the majority of them, originating with the Soviets. Its facilities for accumulating critical information were vast. It was fully aware of Soviet attempts to match CIA penetration of Turkey and Greece. It could identify every agent of Department 8, one of the sixteen divisions of the KGB's First Chief Directorate, whose responsibility was the Arab nations, Albania, Afghanistan, Iran, Yugoslavia, Turkey and Greece. It knew the 'illegals' and was able to uncover a number of 'legal' spies. (A 'legal' agent is a citizen of the country he spies upon. An 'illegal' is a spy in a country of which he is not a citizen.)

Nevertheless, regardless of the CIA's largely defensive, or counter-Intelligence role as a NATO affiliate in the quadrangle, no Intelligence service, and certainly not the Central Intelligence Agency, functions as a defensive organization, and the successful Soviet pseudo-*coup* of 1970, recognized as a test-plan, alerted Intelligence planners to the possibility of additional exacerbation.

Where the difficulty arose in that situation came about as a result, not of the Soviet intrusion, but as a result of the fact that foreign operations could be abundantly successful in the accumulation of hard facts, such as a warning to the Greeks that a Turkish armed invasion of Cyprus was imminent in early 1974, and a warning to the Turks that such an invasion would certainly imperil NATO's southern bastion, with a most sanguinary result: the warnings were ignored.

The agency had to deal with Turkish and Greek leaders whose individuality and ambition were formed by an age-old antagonism; men whose politics were more immediately concerned with Turkish and Greek national issues than with what to them had always been an abstraction—NATO.

The agency, then, with full knowledge of what was inevitable, the Turkish invasion of Cyprus following the Greek-led overthrow of Cyprus's president, Archbishop Makarios, tried to avert the trouble at the same time it warned Washington. It exerted pressure on Greek and Turkish men of power, many of whom it had been financially subsidizing. The United States State Department did the same, but the invasion could not be stopped. Regional politics had ensured it as the Soviets were aware, back in 1970 when they at that time attempted to foment it.

Intelligence analysts offered the one ray of hope, for, while war between Greece and Turkey would certainly have encouraged Soviet political and military penetration, containment would just as surely minimize this danger.

According to the analysts Turkey's invasion force would probably not exceed 5,000 troops, half a dozen escorting warships and an adequate air flotilla to support ground forces, hardly enough power to do more than neutralize the Greek Cypriots and achieve temporary island control.

Intelligence officials became involved in containing that which neither they, the UN, nor the US State Department could prevent, and they were barely successful.

While fighting intensified on the island, efforts were made to negate a far more dangerous situation. In Thrace, where Greek and Turkish troops faced one another across their common boundary, it would have taken very little to start a genuine war. This confrontation was gradually de-escalated despite several episodes of shooting, and over a period of days, then weeks, the danger lessened. Finally, negotiations were inaugurated, a cease-fire was agreed to, and while nothing was actually resolved, and probably never would be to the satisfaction of Greeks, Turks or Cypriots, for the time being at any rate, the historic difficulty had been contained.

For the CIA, whose role throughout had been defensive and placating, the rewards were poor; accused by both sides of interference and duplicity, the agency had no choice but to remain mute to allegations that it had, as an instrument of the United States, abetted the humiliation of Greece, limited the armed ambition of Turkey, and supported the largely unpopular Greek-Cypriot junta of Nikos Sampson.

What the agency *had* done was try to prevent armed trouble, and when it had been unable to do that, it had then worked equally as hard to contain the trouble. In this it had been successful, along with the other involvees including 10 Downing Street, NATO, and the United Nations, but the Intelligence position has almost invariably been suspect. Generally, the consensus has been in accord with a statement made by Nikita Khrushchev in 1962: 'Espionage is needed by those who prepare for attack, for aggression. . . .'

Obviously, too, because espionage involves secrecy, and very often tactics which at the least are unethical and at most are illegal, even the people who recognize the necessity for espionage are uncomfortable about it.

Justification for this attitude exists. There are rules for spies which apply only to them. Betrayal, for example, is equated by most people with treachery or treason. Among professionals of the Intelligence craft betrayal has another name: defection.

Throughout the Greek-Turkish difficulties of 1974–75 CIA informers on both sides fed valuable information to their Intelligence contacts. These people were spies, purely and simply, but the most damaging informers have been those, such as Oleg Penkovskiy and Vladimir Sakharov of the Soviet Union who defected and became CIA agents, or former United States Intelligence personnel such as Philip Agee, among others, who defected in the opposite direction.

Within the past decade there has emerged another variety of defector, the secret agent who has gone public; for example Victor Marchetti, a CIA agent for fourteen years, whose book *The CIA and the Cult of Intelligence*, written in conjunction with John D. Marks, offered a public view of agency organization as well as a thoroughly biased judgement of the Intelligence spectrum.

These 'defectors' are largely responsible for the general disenchantment with an element of government which is as indispensable to national health as is the gross national product.

16

The Hazards of Defection

Whatever the causes for defection may be, and the reasons seem to be as interestingly varied as the kinds of people who defect, without a doubt more people go west than go east.

The establishment of obstacles to defection such as walls, watchtowers, barbed-wire barriers, even mine fields, have not been successful deterrents to people from the USSR or the Communist-bloc nations whose determination has been adequately resolute; however, the kind of defector most valued by Western Intelligence sources rarely has to scale a wall or sneak past a watchtower. He is usually already in the West as an embassy attaché, a KGB agent, or a member of a trade commission, and thus far neither the West nor the East has successfully devised a means for preventing his defection, although there have been a number of such defectors who have not survived their defection long enough to be of much value to their new friends, or to enjoy their freedom.

Walter Krivitsky, for example, a senior Soviet Intelligence officer who defected to the West in 1937 after holding the post of NKVD chief in Holland, was found shot to death in a Washington hotel room. His assassin was never found. In 1962 a Hungarian secret police official, Bela Lapusnyik, defected, and was shortly afterwards found dead of poisoning. There have been many more. Defection is a hazardous undertaking. Those who view turncoats to *their* side as defectors, view their own people who go over to the *other* side as traitors. Historically and traditionally the punishment for treason has been death.

Every Intelligence organization has a special reception procedure for defectors and, as has been previously mentioned, whatever the reason for a defection—disillusionment, disappointment, a desire for vengeance, a preference for one system over the other system—spies who defect seek other spies to defect to.

Since the end of World War II every major Soviet or Bloc defector of note has been connected in some way with Intelligence. If this seems representative of disillusionment in a particular sector, it is not, because every deputation to the West, scientific, cultural, or diplomatic, has either career spies or 'co-opted' (recruited for the time being) agents in its party. In fact, as many as two-thirds of a cultural troupe or an embassy staff, will be KGB people.

A number of Soviet defectors have detailed their experiences as USSR Intelligence agents through the publication of memoirs. Aleksandr Kaznacheev, a 'co-opted' embassy official in Rangoon, told his story through a book entitled *Inside a Soviet Embassy* (Lippincott Company), Peter Deriabin, who defected in Austria, wrote a book in conjunction with Frank Gibney entitled *The Secret World* (Doubleday Company). Gibney and Deriabin collaborated again in 1965 on *The Penkovskiy Papers*, the story of senior Soviet military officer, Colonel Oleg Penkovskiy.

The list is very long and very revealing. Thus far in the East there has not been anywhere nearly as many books by former Western spies, although one such book, *Inside the Company—A CIA Diary*, by Philip Agee, a former divinity student who served the CIA as an ardent field officer for ten years, then changed sides, was published in 1975, and several other 'exposés' have appeared within the past few years, but few books by a Western defector from the Intelligence sector have reached the Russian public, although several patently KGB-scripted 'revelations' have appeared.

It is symptomatic of the differences in the systems that Agee could publish his book in the West, and remain alive and safe from prosecution, but defector Agee, while in contact with the KGB through Cuban and other satellite Intelligence organizations, has thus far avoided visiting the Soviet Union. It is very probable that a strong suspicion of Agee's motives, and perhaps his stability, might incline Soviet Intelligence to withhold a visitor's visa. In any case they have not had to cultivate Agee except indirectly through satellite networks, which absolves them from direct involvement.

Agee is unique among defectors. A United States citizen, although a resident of Cornwall, England, he has not fled to sanctuary. Others have, from both sides, and while the great number of Soviet and satellite defectors have increased Western knowledge of the *details* of Communist espionage, there have been few defectors of Oleg Penkovskiy's calibre; he knew far more than details.

Penkovskiy, whose career as a Soviet war hero, graduate of the Soviet staff college and missile academy, with access to the most secret plans of the Soviet leadership, supplied the CIA with the information which President Kennedy used as the basis for his nerve-wracking confrontation with the USSR in 1962 over emplacement of Soviet missiles in Cuba.

It was Penkovskiy, initially recruited by the British because the Central Intelligence Agency considered him too good to be true, who supplied the West with full information about Russia's nuclear bluff. When President Kennedy challenged Premier Khrushchev over the Cuban missiles, Kennedy knew the Soviets could not risk nuclear war because despite their bombast they did not possess an adequate nuclear capability. Oleg Penkovskiy supplied this information. He also identified for United States Intelligence the missiles in Cuba.

How much more Colonel Penkovskiy revealed remains secret, but, as a CIA double-agent, he returned to the Soviet Union on three separate occasions, and brought out more top-secret Soviet information.

Penkovskiy was motivated, it would appear, by fear that the Soviet Union was being led along the road to an unnecessary and avoidable nuclear war with the West. There appeared to be other reasons: he was fascinated by Western candour and the open societies. He had for years harboured resentment against the Soviet system for its denigration of an aunt, among others in his family who had formerly been petty bourgeois. And Penkovskiy despised then-Premier Nikita Khrushchev.

Seemingly an accumulation of motives, which were about equally divided between harmless and self-destructive impulses, led Oleg Penkovskiy to seek his accommodation with Western Intelligence sources.

His value was considerable, but as a result of his defection to MI6 in 1960 and his subsequent utilization as a joint venture by both MI6 and the CIA, almost any senior Intelligence officer could have made a reasonable prediction about how long he could function, and stay alive. In a society where even the highest officials of government are subject to surveillance, an army colonel, especially one who had visited the West, was a natural, even a very routine, candidate for GRU (Soviet Military Intelligence) and KGB interest.

There were CIA agents within the Soviet Union, some of whom had been there for years, whose ongoing value would be greater if nowhere nearly as spectacular as Penkovskiy's value, simply because they would still be consistently productive long after Colonel Penkovskiy was dead.

Subsequent to the disclosure of Penkovskiy's defection and execution a number of detractors appeared seeking to minimize his disclosures. No rebuttal was required; the facts were rather self-evident that if he had not accomplished anything else—and he certainly *had*, as MI6 and CIA secret files could have proved—he had done something no other Soviet defector, in fact no other Russian defector had ever accomplished: he had brought down a USSR premier.

When the stunned Soviet leadership eventually learned the extent of Penkovskiy's revelations to the West, and how he had undermined Nikita Khrushchev's nuclear blackmail attempts between 1961 and 1962, leaving the Soviet premier looking ridiculous, Penkovskiy was executed and Khrushchev was retired.

Defections from the Communist bloc, great as they have been in other categories, among scientists, writers, military officers, diplomats, cultural and trade personnel, have not all added together equalled defections from the Intelligence sectors: the GRU (*Glavnoye Razvedyvatelnoye Upravleniye*), which is the Soviet military Intelligence organization, the Chief Intelligence Directorate, Soviet General Staff, and the KGB (*Komitet Gosudarstvennoy Bezopasnosti*), the external *and* internal Intelligence and security equivalent to the Central Intelligence Agency, but with far greater power and size.

The odds against Colonel Penkovskiy surviving for any considerable length of time were enormous. The odds against his Western contacts evading disclosure were equally as great.

Greville Wynn, the ostensible English businessman who was arrested at the same time Penkovskiy was apprehended, and who was subsequently exchanged by the Soviets for their Ukrainian master-spy Conon Malody, also known as Gordon Lonsdale, wrote a book with MI6 assistance, entitled *Contact on Gorky Street,* about his experiences, which, from the very beginning, left little doubt about the ultimate outcome. This book, incidentally and no doubt with deliberate intent, coincided with the publication within the Soviet Union of a book by a defector from MI6, the senior Intelligence officer Harold 'Kim' Philby, whose KGB-scripted publication did for Soviet readers what Wynn's book did for the British; it presented a harrowing visualization of how flagrantly dishonest the 'other side' was, and of course must always be.

For Wynn, sentenced to eight years' imprisonment and who actually served a year and a half before being exchanged, there was one cause for a wry smile. At the conclusion of the four-day trial he was presented with a stiff bill for legal services by his Soviet attorney, in the best capitalist tradition.

At the close of the trial the Soviet prosecutor denounced the United States Intelligence effort in these words: 'A leading role in this [affair] belongs to the Central Intelligence Agency of the US—the support of the most adventurist circles in the US. Like a giant octopus it extends its tentacles into all corners of the earth, supports a tremendous number of spies and secret informants . . .' [and employs] 'modern techniques . . . from the miniature Minox cameras which you see before you [in evidence at the trial], to space satellites, "spies in the sky".'

Of MI6 he said: 'The British Intelligence Service, which has been in existence for about three hundred years, is no less insidious and astute in its methods, but it attempts to remain more in the background. . . .'

The *Penkovskiy Papers*, which enjoyed a good reception in Europe and the United States, revealed none of the secrets brought to the West by Colonel Penkovskiy. Like other information of a classified nature delivered by other Soviet and Bloc defectors they will never be made public in their entirety.

Other Soviet and Red Bloc defectors of a much less exalted stature than Colonel Penkovskiy have provided the CIA, as well as corollary Western Intelligence organizations with a voluminous amount of material, and they have not all been spies. For example KGB agent Nikolai Khokhlov, who held the rank of captain and who had been a secret agent for many years, was directed by an order bearing the signatures of Georgi Malenkov and Nikita Kruschev to assassinate a Russian *émigré*, Georgi Sergeevich Okolovich, head of a vocal and politically strong organization known as NTS (*Narodyn-Truduvoy Soyuz*) People's Labour

League), which consisted of Russians living in Germany. Khokhlov, whose background included terrorism, spying and other clandestine activities, could not commit murder, and well aware of the consequences of disobedience, defected.

When the KGB learned that Khokhlov had become a CIA informer, it had him poisoned in a most ingenious manner. He collapsed in Frankfurt and was taken to hospital. His body became discoloured, his hair fell out, blood came through his skin, he could not eat, and his salivary glands ceased to function.

A diagnosis of thallium poisoning was made, but no antidote for this particular variety of poisoning helped, and Khokhlov was pronounced terminally ill. He was taken to a United States military hospital in Frankfurt for additional tests and treatment. Clearly dying, Khokhlov was kept barely alive by intravenous injections. His blood, it was learned, was deteriorating rapidly, as were his bones. Constant blood transfusions and pain deadeners were administered.

An American expert in toxicology discovered how Khokhlov had been poisoned. The thallium in his system had been treated to large doses of atomic radiation, causing the thallium to become infinitesimally pulverized so that it could be absorbed systematically. Khokhlov was dying of deadly radiation poisoning.

He was started on a fresh course of treatment, and although he survived and eventually recovered—with permanent damage—no one was certain how this happened, any more than they were able to discover how, and exactly when, a KGB assassin had reached him.

Nikolai Khokhlov's conscience nearly got him killed. Another KGB assassin and spy, Bogdan Stashinsky, who also defected to the CIA in Germany, had a more belated attack of conscience, with unfortunate consequences for two other *émigrés* living in Germany, Lev Rebet, a fiercely anti-Soviet Ukrainian political figure, and Stefan Bandera, a notorious Ukrainian guerrilla leader during World War II and afterwards who had opposed the Soviets both physically and verbally for years.

Stashinsky, a handsome young man who had been recruited by the KGB before his twentieth birthday, and who spoke German, was flown into Munich to kill Lev Rebet. The murder weapon was a steel tube about eight inches long loaded with a glass cartridge containing prussic acid and operated by simple and noiseless triggering mechanism.

Four days after his arrival in Munich, having located Rebet and having studied Rebet's daily habits, Bogdan Stashinsky knew exactly when his victim would arrive home, and was at the head of the stairs waiting when Rebet entered the building. Stashinsky waited until the unsuspecting Rebet was at the top step, then aimed his tube and depressed the trigger. Lev Rebet staggered and collapsed.

The subsequent autopsy listed the cause of Rebet's death as a heart attack.

Bogdan Stashinsky left Germany, and returned later on another assassination assignment. This time he was required to be more circumspect. Stefan Bandera went armed, was known to be a fearless opponent, and commonly had a bodyguard.

After several weeks of careful preparation, Stashinsky was ready. He found Stefan Bandera alone in his garage and started to approach him. He was suddenly overcome by revulsion at what he was about to do. After a moment of troubled indecision, Stashinsky turned and walked away.

The penalty for failure was unpleasant to contemplate, so when Stashinsky reported to his contact in Karlshorst, he lied; another man had suddenly walked up, Stashinsky said, and his appearance had spoiled the plan.

The lie was accepted, for the time being, but a month later new orders were received instructing Stashinsky immediately to fulfil his assignment. During the interim, however, Stashinsky's conscience had become stronger. He went forth with his steel tube to kill Bandera nevertheless, but arrived at a painful decision. If Stefan Bandera appeared outside his Munich home before one o'clock in the morning he would assassinate him, if not, Stashinsky would return to Karlshorst, confess his deliberate failure and accept punishment.

Accordingly, Stashinsky took up a position near Bandera's building and waited. The fates were unkind to Stefan Bandera. He parked his car out in front of his residence at about ten minutes until one o'clock in the morning. Stashinsky walked over and as Bandera inserted his key into the door-lock, Stashinsky aimed and fired. Stefan Bandera died at 1.05 p.m.

This time the autopsy disclosed prussic acid in the body. Bandera obviously had been murdered, but until Stashinsky defected much later and confessed to both murders, the German police had no idea who the killer had been, although they rationalized that the Bandera killing had been political.

Bogdan Stashinsky was personally awarded the Order of the Red Banner by Alexander N. Shelepin, at that time chairman of the KGB, and subsequently a high Soviet diplomat. Shelepin was —and is—a notorious hater of the United States.

Defection by Westerners from the Intelligence community, negligible in proportion to Soviet and Red Bloc Intelligence defections, nevertheless occurs, but no high CIA officials has defected to the Soviets, and excluding Kim Philby the British have been equally as fortunate. In general, though, both nations have had their share of defectors outside Intelligence, for example John Vassal, the English Admiralty clerk convicted in 1962 of spying for the USSR, and the Rosenbergs, Julius and Ethel, in the United States, who were sentenced to death and executed as Soviet spies.

There is a third category of defector. It consists of people who are professional 'defectors' and who are double agents for one side or the other. They normally run a greater risk than genuine defectors or loyal spies. Some, uniquely enough, have served the CIA as spies 'in place', and as 'legals', having been recruited in their respective nations, and when they have defected have done so on CIA orders. Commonly, these people have not been known outside the CIA as having been spies; when they 'defected' they did so as scientists, teachers, embassy personnel. There could accrue no value at all from disclosing that they had also been spies.

The obvious opportunities for infiltrating agents into a country under the guise of defectors has long been an available practice, but in this respect most of the advantage has been with the Soviets, who are notoriously chary of all defectors, and have kept them under close surveillance with limited access even to Soviet stores and public transportation facilities, without respite, sometimes all their lives. In this respect, at least, it has been true that closed societies have been difficult to penetrate.

On the other hand KGB infiltration of Western nations has flourished, and this has required of the CIA an immense and costly counter-Intelligence effort. With the cut-back of MI6's budget, and the elimination of any great need by the British to be as vitally concerned in all areas of the world as they once were, the CIA has been required to expand its facilities. Aside from Northern Ireland and Britain itself, MI6 has now a limited scope as the result of an abbreviated national interest, nevertheless it has been through the expertise of MI6 that many pseudo-defectors have been uncovered. MI6 agents have had a most unsettling capacity for appearing in places and under circumstances where other Intelligence organizations have not expected to find them. In the Maurice Dejean affair (Chapter 17) in which the KGB employed the oldest of all 'dirty tricks', sexual entrapment of a French ambassador to the Soviet Union, a matter which would normally have been handled secretly and exclusively between Moscow and Paris, it was MI6 which discreetly informed the French of the entire affair. They had no prior knowledge of it at all.

MI6's capacity for uncovering imitation defectors to the West earned the CIA's admiration, but since most KGB 'plants' have been aimed at the United States over the past two decades, responsibility for uncovering them has been almost entirely a CIA function.

What has made it most difficult has been not only the great numbers of defectors, but the identical excuses they all offer as their reasons for defection; impossible assignments with the certainty of punishment for failure, frustrated ambition, disagreement with policies of the state for which there exist no safe means for openly disagreeing, fascination with the freedom of Western societies, lack of proper recognition or merit, hatred of oppression, fear, even religious tendencies. They are all standard reasons. They are also valid reasons. The KGB has used them all, and still uses them. The logical defence, aside from a hard background investigation which is conducted in all cases in any event, lies in the same kind of persevering suspicion which the Soviets employ. Otherwise, of course, there is the polygraph and other technological testing devices, but ultimately what is buried in a defector's brain—or a spy's brain—will be revealed through his actions, and that takes time to discover, and meanwhile the defector, if he belongs to the category of pseudos, will be at work.

There is another problem for the CIA. Two problems, actually. By law the agency is not allowed to undertake counter-Intelligence functions within the national boundaries of the United States.

Once a defector reaches sanctuary in the United States he becomes an *internal*, not an *external* risk, and internal security is the FBI's responsibility.

The second problem is more chilling to professional Intelligence people. One out of every twenty-seven residents of the United States is an illegal alien.

Even if the FBI had the funds to cope with a dilemma of this magnitude it would not have the manpower. In fact if the FBI and the CIA were combined into one internal-external national security agency, like the KGB, it would still not have the manpower to thoroughly investigate and watch nearly eight million people.

17

Entrapment

Cliché or not the term 'sexual entrapment' remains today as valid as it ever was. The same kind of prostitutes are employed, and the same variety of pigeons queue up to be plucked.

If there has been any progress in the hoary routine it perhaps lies in terminology. It has been a long time since anyone abashedly said a girl named Delilah cut off the hair of a man named Samson thus robbing him of his strength. Especially within the last decade or two. It is rarely even called seduction any more, which was a middle-of-the-road approach, somewhere between Samson's symbolic 'shearing' and the pungent no-nonsense oldtime Saxon word. But regardless of the noun employed or the techniques involvéd to achieve an entrapment, the ends are no different now than they were when the seventh Cleopatra, last of the Ptolemies, dallied with Julius Caesar from October to June, 47 B.C., which should have weakened him as it subsequently did Samson, but apparently Caesar's recuperative capabilities were superior because he went on to conquer Asia Minor, defeat his opponents beyond Carthage, and also to vanquish Spain.

Perhaps emperors possessed more stamina than ordinary statesmen. Be that as it may, the techniques of employing sexual entrapment remained fundamentally unaltered. In the 1960s and 1970s the CIA, the KGB, and most probably MI6 as well as the French and German Intelligence services utilized this time-hallowed, quite dependable means for either blackmailing enemies, as in the Dejeans matter, or of destroying them, as in the Courtney affair.

Royal Navy Commander Anthony Courtney, a widowered Member of Parliament noted for his outspoken scepticism of the Soviet Union and his totally realistic advocacy of a hard-handed method of dealing with KGB infiltration, and the abuse of diplomatic privilege by the Soviets within the United Kingdom, was considered by the Soviet Intelligence services as a major threat to Soviet penetration. They accordingly engaged in a systematic, in-depth evaluation. Commander Courtney was a large, physically powerful man. He had at one time been the heavyweight champion boxer of the Royal Navy. He was fearless, intelligent, absolutely realistic, and of course virile. In 1961 he toured the USSR, and the intourist guide assigned to him was Zinaida Grigorievna Volkova, who was no Cleopatra but she was attractive and personable. Widower Anthony Courtney, while not overwhelmed by Zinaida Volkova, was not recalcitrant either when she called upon him one evening, after working hours. What ensued was a liaison between two unattached and consenting adults. It also happened to be a matter of interest to the KGB and its proficient photographer.

Four years passed. Commander Courtney did not see or hear from Zinaida Volkova again. During that period Courtney remarried. In 1965 he brought to the attention of Parliament the matter of Soviet and satellite abuses of diplomatic privilege for the purposes of espionage and subversion in Great Britain. He organized a considerable Tory following in support of his demands that a proper investigation be made with the objective being a reduction of Soviet and Red Bloc embassy personnel.

The KGB brought forth its Courtney dossier, had copies made of the embarrassing photographs of Commander Courtney and Zinaida Volkova and posted them to Courtney's second wife, various publications, and Members of Parliament. They were also reprinted in several magazines and sent to several foreign embassies.

When Courtney was required to offer a defence, he did so exactly in accordance with the facts, and when he stood for reelection to Parliament in 1966, he lost badly. It of course did nothing for Commander Courtney's cause that Britain had not yet recovered from the sex-scandal surrounding the fall of War Minister John Profumo, which had occurred only a short time earlier.

It was said at that time that Anthony Courtney should have anticipated the results of his momentary dalliance, and perhaps he should have, but it is also a fact that hindsight is more common than foresight.

Another KGB entrapment which succeeded in destroying a man's career, and which also cost another man his life, involved a close associate of the late French President Charles De Gaulle. His name was Maurice Dejean and at the time of this interlude Dejean was fifty-six years of age, married to Marie-Claire, and was the French ambassador to the USSR.

The Soviets, who had an extensive file on Maurice Dejean, were fully aware of his close friendship with De Gaulle, which went back to the troubled days of the Second World War. Their interest in Dejean was based upon the ambassador's steady rise to power over the years, and their expectation that he would continue to achieve high office.

Perhaps because Dejean was a more politically prestigious individual than Commander Courtney the plot against him was more elaborate. But it was also just as hackneyed and heavy-handed.

A KGB agent, Yuri Vasilevitch Krotkov, a handsome man with a background in drama and the theatre, was assigned to the seduction of Marie-Claire Dejean. Krotkov had previously been employed in this role against other foreign women living in the USSR. He worked assiduously for more than a year, and while Madame Dejean became fond of Krotkov, she avoided his ardent overtures so well that the KGB was compelled to abandon this aspect of the project.

They were more successful with the ambassador. A strikingly handsome actress, Lydia Khovanskaya ultimately enticed Monsieur Dejean to her apartment, and during the two-hour interlude which followed, monitored of course by the KGB, Maurice Dejean was photographed in the course of some very sprightly calisthenics with Lydia Khovanskaya.

But Khovanskaya was not the woman for whom Ambassador Dejean formed his attachment. That was Larissa Kronberg-Sobolevskaya, an uninhibited actress, statuesque in build, ebullient by nature, and notoriously ardent. Lydia Khovanskaya was withdrawn from the assignment through a plausible excuse—she had to leave Moscow to work in a picture then under production—and Maurice Dejean became infatuated with hard-drinking Larissa, who was also known as Lora. Their affair became a matter of the utmost importance to Dejean, and when his wife returned for a visit to France Dejean and Lora became practically inseparable—with the KGB accumulating some interesting film footage.

Then came the *dénouement*, exactly on schedule in the finest tradition of oldtime burlesque. Lora's outraged 'husband' arrived home unexpectedly from his work in Siberia, and over the heart-rending lamentations of the disrobed Lora, began immediately to berate her as a faithless wanton while simultaneously punching the equally as disgracefully disrobed Dejean, and all the while in the adjoining room KGB officials and photographers were observing what was a slightly kinky ending to a plot as old as melodrama, and older.

Lora's 'husband' threatened Dejean with exposure, and since Dejean was in the Soviet Union, with friends there in high office, he confided his dilemma to one such friend, Oleg Gribanov, completely unaware that the friend to whom he appealed for help had been one of the observers in the adjoining room a short while earlier. Dejean's 'friend' was KGB General Oleg Mikhailovitch Gribanov.

After an appropriate lapse of time, during which Madame Dejean returned from France to discover her husband in a nervous, agitated condition, Gribanov informed the ambassador that he had, through much effort and diligent application, managed to hush up the entire matter, and to also placate Lora's outraged husband.

At no time did Gribanov mention reciprocal favours. The Soviets had not effected their entrapment of Ambassador Dejean in order to blackmail him about French military or diplomatic secrets. They had done it for the same reason they had compromised Commander Courtney: to have a devastating file complete with erotic photographs to be used at some future date, perhaps when Maurice Dejean was a high minister of France.

Dejean's air attaché, Colonel Louis Gibaud, who was also lured into entrapment, reacted quite differently when he was confronted by the KGB with the customary erotic photographs. But in the Gibaud matter the KGB wanted immediate collaboration; Colonel Gibaud was to accept recruitment as a spy, and upon returning to France was to become a 'legal' for the KGB.

Gibaud went to his office at the embassy and there shot himself, and was found dead on the floor, service pistol at his side.

For one of the conspirators, who was not experienced in this aspect of the trade of subversion, Yuri Krotkov, Gibaud's suicide was a terrible shock. Compromising a man, courting an ambassador's wife, being part of seduction conspiracies, were things Krotkov could act out with no great pains of conscience, but to deliberately drive a man to kill himself was an appalling thing.

Krotkov was in a group of Soviet dramatists who landed at Heathrow Airport in the first week of September 1963. On 12th September Krotkov sauntered from his hotel, journeyed to Hyde Park, and that same night MI6 officials sat in stony silence as Yuri Krotkov told them of the Dejean affair, and why Louis Gibaud had taken his life.

MI6 alerted the French, a counter-Intelligence official also interrogated Krotkov, then promptly flew to France for an urgent meeting behind closed doors with the highest officials of France. Subsequently, after a suitably corroborating investigation had been concluded, Maurice Dejean was personally dismissed from high office by Charles De Gaulle.

Yuri Vasilevitch Krotkov eventually did what every amoral penitent who flees the Soviet Union seeks to do. First, he wrote a book about his experiences in the Soviet Union, and being a changed man, now full of ethics and morality, he did not mention anywhere in his book that he had ever been connected with the KGB.

Krotkov's second little triumph was to emigrate to the United States where, in 1969, he told a Senatorial Security Subcommittee what he knew of the Dejean affair.

Finally, Yuri Krotkov undertook to pursue a new life in the United States based upon a seeking for peace, and a meeting with God. His chances were probably as remote for finding one as for contacting the other, particularly in Washington or New York.

The examples of Courtney, Dejean, and Louis Gibaud, unhappily sordid though they were, emphasized that the oldest kind of entrapment—sexual—still flourished practically unchanged in its *modus operandi* from earliest times, which could conceivably lend emphasis to someone's apophthegm that perfection need not be improved upon.

It might also explain why the Central Intelligence Agency, whose finesse and expertise in other fields suggested a hypothetical superiority in many areas, did no better in this particular speciality of Intelligence suborning and subversion than did the KGB.

It has been said that the CIA imitated KGB entrapment procedures, a patent falsehood since the stylized routine for sexual entrapment has existed basically unchanged for several thousand years. It exploits an instinctive impulse, and there has never been anything required beyond a convenient availability to ensure that success ensues.

For almost ten years the CIA operated several 'safe houses' in California, at San Francisco, for the purpose of having convenient residences available where foreigners could be lured by entrapment. The 'pick-ups' were made by both male and female prostitutes in the agency's employ.

In New York where similar establishments were operated until about 1967, conveniently close to United Nations facilities, complete with one-way mirrors in the walls of adjoining apartments, photographic facilities and sound-track installations, the opportunities for suborning and blackmail were extensive and quite successful. But in an open society where people could loudly proclaim indignation over such invasions of privacy, while actually being acutely embarrassed at the thought of personally appearing on closed-circuit television frenetically bouncing in naked ecstasy, the agency could not be as brusquely impervious as the KGB had been. Therefore the CIA's entrapment procedures, while undeviating in the basics, required a more sophisticated approach; for example, to avoid discovery as proprietor of these apartments, the CIA arranged with another agency, one whose normal function was narcotics control, to pay the rent, sign the leases, buy the liquor and groceries, and otherwise use the apartments so that they would have a lived-in appearance. When a CIA entrapment was in process the other agency would be given notice to vacate. Afterwards, its personnel were again at liberty to enjoy the apartments. How the other agency used them was debatable. At least one narcotics official in California had—still has—a son who has been apprehended as a narcotics user and seller.

The CIA had files on every foreigner. Those selected for entrapment were tempted by prostitutes whose speciality coincided with the sexual desires of the victim. How successful all this was remains impossible to determine.

Undoubtedly it *was* successful. Undoubtedly, too, the very secret entrapment programme in San Francisco and New York, closed in the mid and late 1960s, were not abandoned. It could be assumed with reasonable safety that since these were satisfactorily productive tools of the Intelligence craft, if they were closed in one area they were certainly reactivated in another area.

As for their morality, which seems to be where all critics stop in their analyses of the subject, leaving the judgement—and the titillating imaginings—to their audiences, there remains something to be said which is also as old, and probably older, than entrapment itself. It is called free choice or individual prerogative or instinctive compulsion or private initiative.

No one is required to submit to entrapment, sexual or any other kind. It is not basically a coercive instrument. The diplomat or attaché in a foreign country who is lured into some variety of Intelligence snare, but particularly a sexual one, is a voluntary dupe, and if this does not alter the fact that a foreign Intelligence apparatus takes advantage of him, there is certainly justification, and it has nothing to do with President Ford's fatuous remark that because 'they' do it, 'we' also do it.

Human motivations, needs, desires, weaknesses and strengths are commonplace aspects of every phase of the daily human experience, and the infinitely more immoral individuals whose philosophy is grounded in vaster programmes of subjugation and entrapment—Hitler, Stalin, Mussolini, so forth—and who exploit those human motivations in order to accomplish mental or physical enslavement, deserve to be opposed and are opposed.

In the interests of survival and defence the weapons as well as the tools are available. For the West it is not a question of what the 'other side' does. It is a question of what the West must do to survive and remain free. If this requires the exploitation of human frailties, then they will be exploited, and it is not as though these exploitations result from an application of thumbscrews or strappado; no one is forced into bed, they go there voluntarily. If they choose not to be entrapped, they have the privilege of avoiding a horizontal position.

18

Counter-Intelligence

The counter-Intelligence aspect of espionage is defensive, otherwise all espionage is offensive. Counter-espionage is the system by which an Intelligence organization defends itself while simultaneously seeking to penetrate similar attempts at defence by foreign Intelligence organizations.

All espionage is complicated but counter-Intelligence can become unbelievably involved. It has not been unusual for the CIA to uncover a KGB spy, recruit him, feed information through him to the KGB and have the recruited double agent re-defect which would make him a triple agent, then begin feeding disinformation back to the CIA.

Counter-espionage has the responsibility of exposing double agents. A most plausible way to do this has been to photograph the agent at a rendezvous with a known alien contact. Double agents are necessary to any successful penetration of alien Intelligence systems. They are the spearhead of any attempt at penetration, and every Intelligence organization has constantly to assume it is under such secret attack at the same time it is also launching its own similar attacks.

False defectors have been a counter-espionage responsibility for many years. The CIA's record for uncovering secret agents seeking to infiltrate by this deception is very good. It is also known that one out of every three CIA spies will be caught. In the past many were executed. Since the inauguration of the exchange system it can be expected that shooting and garroting, the Communist methods of disposal, may become less commonplace.

Counter-espionage penetration has always been very difficult, and yet it is known that the CIA has been very successful at placing agency spies inside KGB networks. KGB affiliates in Chile in 1970 were thoroughly penetrated, while in reverse the Communists made very little headway with secret CIA networks, although so blatant did the CIA's overthrow effort become that in time every Chilean newspaper knew there was a vast CIA involvement.

Among the most successful operations to arise from counter-espionage have been exposures of alien penetration *in time*. The information gained by the CIA through this means of counter-espionage is called counter-Intelligence.

If in the process of exposure an agent can be recruited, all the better, but the most endangered of all spies is the recruited foreign (double) agent. Nevertheless he may also become an enormously valuable acquisition.

For example, back in 1955 the Soviets became interested in an Egyptian of nondescript appearance named Sami Sharaf, at that time a minor dignitary of an Egyptian aid mission to Moscow.

Subsequently Egyptian cabinet chief Ali Sabry, thought in many Intelligence circles to belong to the KGB, acquired Sami Sharaf as his assistant. Did the Soviets recruit Sami Sharaf in Moscow during his 1955 visit? If so, and if they then interjected him into Ali Sabry's office, it was a sound move. Sami Sharaf gradually expanded his position beyond Ali Sabry until he achieved influence with the man who ruled Egypt in 1959, Gamal Abdul Nasser. By this time Sharaf had made another trip to the Soviet Union. He also visited the United States, in 1958. In 1959 he emerged as President Nasser's trusted Intelligence adviser leaving Ali Sabry far behind. He got KGB information from case-officer Vadim Kipichenko which he fed to President Nasser.

In 1960 and 1961 Sami Sharaf's influence had reached a very influential level, among other duties he supervised an élite 'place guard' of secret agents whose duty was to spy within the government as well as within the foreign diplomatic community and report exclusively to Sharaf. Additionally, Sharaf had by this time achieved almost total control of all Intelligence seen by President Nasser. As a controlled Soviet agent, which he clearly was and had been since perhaps as early as 1955 or 1958, Sami Sharaf made it possible for the Soviets to manipulate the President of Egypt.

To augment an illusion of espionage expertise which the Egyptians never possessed, a number of Bloc spies 'defected' 'in place' as double agents serving Egypt—which they were not serving at all. Their job was to feed anti-American information to the Egyptians.

This entire scheme had been very carefully created in order that the Soviet Union could, when the time was thought to be appropriate, accomplish penetration of Egypt at the very highest level. It had been tried before, never successfully, in places such as Turkey, Jordan, Mexico and Guatemala. It came unnervingly close to succeeding in Egypt.

By 1967 with Gamal Abdul Nasser's life drawing to a close, the second most powerful man in Egypt was Sami Sharaf. He was the only high executive not thought in Egyptian circles to be in Soviet pay. Minister of War Mohammed Fauzi was known to be a Soviet dupe, as was Vice President Ali Sabry who had been under Soviet domination for years, Sharawi Gomaa, Minister of the Interior was a Soviet pawn. That only left two loyal nationalists, President Nasser and his most trusted adviser, advocate of Arab unity, Sami Sharaf.

When war clouds appeared in the Middle East Sami Sharaf delivered to President Nasser KGB disinformation to convince Nasser that the British, Americans, and the French were going to abandon Egypt at the last moment and support Israel in a war of attrition. Finally, when war came in the Middle East the Soviets knew when and where the initial strikes would occur but deliberately withheld that information for their own reasons and contributed in this manner to Egypt's humiliating defeat. Why? Because well before 1970 it was possible to subvert the free nation of Egypt into a Socialist Republic of Egypt, as much a Soviet proprietory nation as Hungary, Czechoslovakia or Poland. What was required was national demoralization—the vacuum—a set of leaders owned by the USSR and a president susceptible to Soviet influence and pressure. No one will ever know how close success came. President Nasser died in the eleventh hour and a new man, Anwar Sadat, came to power.

The entire undertaking had to be restructured to accommodate a new dupe, Sadat. Trouble came almost immediately. Anwar Sadat would not be bought, influenced or coerced. He was an Egyptian nationalist with no detectable leanings towards either the East or West, and consequently the Soviet scheme which had come within a hair's breadth of being attempted and very possibly succeeding, faltered.

In April, 1971 Sami Sharaf among other important Egyptians visited Moscow. Grave discussions by these people and the KGB resulted in a decision that because Sadat could not be swayed he would have to be disposed of, otherwise all the years of careful and expensive scheming which had come so close to success prior to Nasser's demise, would have to be abandoned, something the KGB and the MFA (Ministry of Foreign Affairs) would not consider.

Egypt had been penetrated to the highest level. Any time an alien Intelligence organization could control the information a national chief executive used to form his judgements from, a *coup* was imminent, Egypt had been penetrated superbly. The *coup* was imminent and Anwar Sadat was to be the first casualty.

Penetration was a two-way street, and what now occurred stunned the Soviets. Without warning Anwar Sadat struck. Sami Sharaf, Egypt's chief of Intelligence, along with Ministers Mahommed Fauzi, Ali Sabry, and Sharawi Gomaa, were arrested. Altogether President Sadat uncovered over ninety conspirators. His information of the plot to dispose of him came through a CIA agent within the Moscow KGB apparatus. Those who penetrated Egypt had themselves been penetrated; the name of the game was counter-espionage.

In the Central Intelligence Agency counter-espionage is under the Director of Operations—Clandestine Services. Operations has been spectacularly successful in all its areas—covert action, foreign infiltration, programmes and services—but in counter-espionage its record has been especially noteworthy. Despite a claim of Marks and Marchetti (previously cited) that the 'CIA has had almost no success in penetrating Soviet and other opposition services', the exact opposite is true. One example out of dozens is the case of a Soviet Intelligence officer who served in Yemen as acting Soviet council, who was in fact decorated in Moscow for standing firm when a crowd of 2,000 screaming Yeminis stormed the Soviet Embassy, and who later served in Kuwait and Egypt as a senior KGB officer. His name was Vladimir Nikolaevich Sakharov and he was an 'in place' CIA agent for a number of years.

The list is very long. CIA counter-espionage has demonstrated an excellent ability for establishing counter-espionage implants. It has also been successful in uncovering the links between CIA defectors and their alien contacts. Philip Agee, for example, mentioned earlier, whose claim that he exposed former CIA associates and plans because he viewed the agency as a Fascist organization (which he served well for twelve years), turned out to be somewhat different from the image of an idealist he projected.

Agee publicly exposed the chief of the Communist party in Ecuador as a CIA agent. He also claimed three Mexican presidents were in CIA employ. What he did *not* do was expose Communist agents or plans although clearly he knew quite a bit about both. The reason he did not had less to do with Agee's idealism than it had to do with his defection. During 1971–1972 Agee secretly met Communist agents in Paris. During that same period Agee made four trips to Havana where he was voluntarily debriefed by officials of Cuba's *Dirección General de Inteligencia* (DGI), against whom Agee had worked as a counter-agent for so many years. The DGI is the KGB's Cuban Intelligence affiliate.

Agee's most difficult achievement was convincing the KGB that he was not a counter-espionage plant. Any known CIA agent, but particularly one with Philip Agee's twelve-year record as an active opponent of Communism, would never be able entirely to overcome a suspicion that he was not in fact a double agent.

Agee announced support of the Cuban revolution. He also turned out to be a hard drinker and a man chronically short of funds, until about 1973. He went to Spain in December of 1974, to Canada in 1975, and also made contacts in London with an alien agent. Agee later came to Britain from which his deportation was ordered by the Home Secretary in November 1976 and confirmed after representations against the order, in the House of Commons in February 1977.

Agee's movements were screened, and his pronouncements catalogued, but his successful betrayal was without question and regardless of the CIA's efforts to muzzle it, the most thorough CIA exposé ever. Counter-espionage did not manage to stop publication of Agee's book nor prevent Agee from talking.

For the counter-espionage sector Philip Agee has constituted the most spectacular migraine in years, but most certainly not the only one, and with the passing of time Agee will fade while another phase of defensive spying, domestic activity, will not fade, but will without a doubt become a more enduring embarrassment since it violates the 1947 founding charter.

Domestic spying, Americans spying upon Americans, has been categorized as the worst crime of counter-espionage. It has also been justified among Intelligence services as essential to the welfare and defence of the United States, which it may well be but it is still forbidden by law.

However, there remains Section 102 of the National Security Act of 1947 which has not been extensively invoked by the agency although it probably will be in any final confrontation. The CIA shall perform 'other functions and duties' as directed. On the basis of those few words domestic spying as well as paramilitary adventures in south-east Asia have been authorized and performed.

Technically, the congressmen, clergymen, senators and newspeople who have sought to make publicity footage by being outraged over violation of the agency's charter have been outraged for the wrong reason. It was never a question of the agency's right by charter or law to read mail, infiltrate radical groups or mount paramilitary campaigns, it was the morality of those things.

For all the exasperation he caused CIA chief William Colby and others Philip Agee will survive. By 1977 he will be entirely anachronistic; nothing ages faster than espionage information. On the other hand domestic counter-espionage and additional issues impingeing upon CIA ethics will not go away. Nor can it be expected that even the people who might subscribe to the notion that domestic counter-espionage is closely allied to national security, will feel easy knowing they may also be on one of the agency's lists. (Records Integration—'RI'—the general list, or the 'Staff D' list of people who have been identified as being part of or associated with questionable organizations and causes.)

Again, the cause for outrage has hardly warranted the furore. The Bureau of Internal Revenue has more extensive, complete and revealing records of Americans than all CIA lists combined and has for many years conducted secret spying campaigns on United States citizens with the knowledge of national leaders and lawmakers.

As for domestic CIA counter-espionage, which has been claimed by many practically to blanket the entire United States, the facts are a little less horrendous. Between 1967–68 the agency penetrated several anti-war radical groups on the United States east coast. Agents were infiltrated by White House direction as a result of a belief that alien funds and organizers were supporting the groups.

Surveillance of known dissidents was undertaken. So was wire-tapping and occasionally, burglary. CIA people thought to be peddling classified information to the news media, along with those known to have received and published that information were watched in order to identify their contacts.

The agency took a hard line towards some domestic dissidents, but its actual domestic operation was quite small. Surveillance, which appeared to be the main cause for anxiety among United States look-under-the-bedders, was scarcely worth the cost of exposure. If only a third of the active troublemakers and enemy counterspies in the United States were to be watched, the CIA could not have accomplished it because there were not that many CIA agents.

In 1969 the Justice Department delivered to the CIA nearly 10,000 names of leftists, militants and other kinds of dissidents which had come to the attention of Justice's domestic disturbance bureau. Of these names the agency identified a fraction as likely to be genuinely dangerous. They were watched. Mail going to the Soviet Union, the People's Republic of China and other enemy states was read, copied if valuable, re-sealed and sent on its way.

Once in 1971, a scheme to kill the Vice-President was uncovered through domestic counter-espionage. It was effectively 'dismantled'. In January of 1975, President Gerald Ford, prodded by a vocal press, inaugurated fresh procedures for investigating all CIA activity, domestic and foreign. Subsequently a panel was created and a lengthy five-month investigation was undertaken which culminated in early June of 1975 with an announcement by Vice-President Nelson Rockefeller that the agency had in fact committed some illegal acts but they were few, and predictably an ambitious politician, in this case Senator Frank Church of Idaho denounced Rockefeller's announcement and as chairman of another panel, the Senate Select Committee investigating the Central Intelligence Agency, promised to reveal all, including allegations that the agency was involved in secret murder. (See Chapter 19.)

Inevitably panels come and panels go, their purpose noble and their cost excessive. They may even result in additional enactments of legislation which will prohibit CIA involvement in domestic espionage, but during all their relentless idealism they probably will quite overlook something current drum-thumping politicians, newsmen and academicians have not mentioned during all the uproar over CIA files on about 10,000 United States citizens.

The Federal Bureau of Investigation, unchallenged because it has been empowered by law to spy on United States nationals, has the largest compilation of secret information on Americans in the world. The CIA's paltry list of 10,000 names is scarcely worth considering when compared to the FBI lists. If politicians and newsmakers concerned with allegations of 'invasion of privacy' were seriously to study FBI printouts complete to sexual preferences of millions of United States citizens, they could not avoid feeling chagrined over having gone gnat-hunting in the CIA's perserve, shotgun in hand, while in the FBI's preserve a true carnivore remained alive and well.

The real cause for large-scale and vituperative condemnation of CIA counter-espionage was never domestic spying, it was the revelation during those final calamitous weeks of the Nixon-Watergate *débâcle* that every major participant in the Watergate affair either was or had been affiliated with the Central Intelligence Agency.

This, not surveillance of some irresponsibly immature actress named Fonda whose anti-Americansim had already alienated most citizens, was what appalled people; that a President of the United States could and would use a powerful federal agency deliberately to break the law, sparked the real anti-campaign. Nor could the agency plausibly deny its implication; counter-espionage had achieved some kind of apex in the United States under President Richard Nixon, and Watergate was the result.

Nothing, including Agee's exposé or KGB harassment, hurt the CIA's image with the United States public as much as the Watergate scandal.

19

'Dirty Tricks'

The majority of CIA Intelligence work is not directly concerned with Clandestine Services, also known as 'dirty tricks'.

During the south-east Asia involvement the exact opposite was true, and currently the Intelligence image has largely to do with well-funded, immensely experienced international networks composed largely—mostly in fact—of very sophisticated men who appear quietly in crowds and using silencers assassinate people, or otherwise through more lurid methods topple governments and discreetly influence events.

It is not an entirely erroneous image except for the part about assassination. The Soviet KGB calls it 'wet affairs' (*Mokroye delo*), and has an entire department devoted to it and at times actually uses assassination as a threat, but the Central Intelligence Agency has avoided assassination, although at the first hint of denials detractors immediately resurrect the most recently fallen head of state Chile's Salvador Allende, which may be very ironic because although the agency organized and supervised Allende's fall, the man himself was to escape to Cuba. He was shot to death by Chileans who were not in the agency's employ, and who were caught up in the wild excitement of the overthrow's last, stark hours.

It has also been alleged that the agency has schemed to kill Cuba's Fidel Castro. Many of these allegations have come from Castro himself. One of the infamous Watergate burglars with earlier agency connections, E. Howard Hunt, said that in former times he advocated killing Castro. He also recounted that his proposal was rejected. Another former agent, Frank Sturgis, even went so far as to organize an assassination attempt and launch it, and at the last minute with Premier Castro in the assassin's sights, the project was cancelled.

President Kennedy who was Castro's favourite enemy, once evidently considered ordering an assassination attempt, but at the last minute this undertaking like all others was cancelled. (The Soviet Union also considered killing Castro in 1961 for insubordination, and again in 1968. These plans too were cancelled.)

If the CIA, acting under orders from the White House or through the National Security Council had ever seriously undertaken the assassination of Castro he would be dead today.

Some years back subsequent to an actual physical invasion of the Dominican Republic by Cuban troops, the late Generalíssimo Rafael Leonides Trujillo hired an assassin to kill Castro. The plot was well advanced before the United States learned of it. United States officials immediately contacted Trujillo and demanded he abandon the plot. They also contacted the assassin who was a native of the United States middle west. He was permitted to keep the one-half fee he had collected in advance (over a hundred thousand dollars) and was sent home.

Allegations concerning assassination attempts against Fidel Castro have proliferated out of all proportion to the man's importance—except to Castro. Any time the CIA might have wished to waste Fidel Castro it would have done so. The fact that Castro remains alive is a tribute to the agency's resolve to keep him that way. There is no nation on earth as thoroughly CIA-penetrated as Communist Cuba, nor one with so many zealous, implacable enemies of its leadership living in such numbers so close to its national borders. Neither Cuba's DGI or the USSR's KGB could guarantee Castro's life for one month without CIA support.

Nevertheless there have been lurid tales of the agency's supposed malevolent decades-old wish to either kill Fidel Castro or to have him killed. Enterprising newsmen have 'uncovered' an almost endless variety of plots and assassins including one which implies that the CIA contacted the Mafia to have Cuba's premier assassinated, basing this on the contention that the agency could conceal its own part in the killing by using the Mafia.

Understandably, since Castro was never assassinated despite the innumerable opportunities, as well as the equally numerous people who have wished him dead for so many years, one cannot help but wonder what, precisely kept him alive, unless it was the CIA, and the answer lies among the never-revealed secrets which followed United States-USSR negotiations over withdrawal of Soviet missiles from Cuba. Two promises by the United States guaranteed Castro's continuation. One was to the effect that the United States would not use force (again) in an attempt to oust the Communists. The other was that the United States would not plan, or assist in the planning or execution of, any scheme to kill Fidel Castro.

It is unique that this topic has achieved such priority in discussions of the CIA's clandestine operations. It does not even belong in that category. It would be better to resurrect the Achmed Sukarno affair of 1958 in Indonesia, except that it occurred so long ago that it hardly warrants fresh interest.

Nonetheless, during Dwight Eisenhower's tenure as United States chief executive, while Allen Dulles was CIA director it was decided to aid a force of rebellious islanders at Sumatra in their attempt to oust Indonesia's head of state, Achmed Sukarno, who had gone to great lengths to alienate the United States.

CIA aircraft supported insurgent land and sea operations. President Sukarno told the world the United States was behind the rebels, and both Director Dulles and President Eisenhower categorically denied this in public, with the salutary result that at least for a while the world believed Dulles and Eisenhower. Then on 18th May 1958 Indonesians downed an insurgent B-26. The pilot, taken alive, was an American named Allen Pope. The United States immediately claimed that Pope was an independent individual who had hired his talents to the rebels. Not very many people believed this, and subsequently not very many people believed the earlier Dulles and Eisenhower disclaimers either.

One of the awkward results of the Allen Pope affair was that even while the United States through the CIA was actively supporting Indonesia's insurgents in their war, in order to save the life of Allen Pope the United States was also bartering rice, arms, and money to the Sukarno government.

As a political affair the insurgency against Sukarno was a failure and prior to the undertaking some CIA prognosticators had predicted those exact results based upon thorough and dispassionate analyses.

As a clandestine affair, however, it was fairly representative. It followed traditional guidelines which called for a number of dove-tailing covert actions directed towards one major effect.

Commonly there have been adequate nuclei—in Indonesia it was ground and sea forces—but rarely has there been an adequate air umbrella, a sound propaganda infiltration effort, or enough money. The CIA's participation has been to co-ordinate what already existed with what the agency would supply. All the disparate efforts co-ordinated towards one major effect, should, providing the planning was soundly comprehensive, ensure victory. It did not invariably work out that way. Quite a number of clandestine undertakings failed, and for any number of reasons, but exactly as the classical covert action had guidelines to ensure success, so also were there other guidelines which worked against success. For example, the CIA was not a United States armed force. There were specific limitations which prevented it from acting as an official armed force.

Even during the south-east Asian conflict involving all United States armed and clandestine services, the CIA remained separate. It waged a different kind of war. There were limitations beyond which it could only go providing it was specifically directed to do so. The agency did not have access to the army's sophisticated weaponry except upon a request-granted basis.

The negative guidelines, which created no great problems in south-east Asia, did create problems elsewhere. Indonesia was an example. So was Cuba where a CIA clandestine effort, already limited by those adverse guidelines, was turned into a disaster because of restrictive factors. United States fighter aircraft could at any time have emptied Cuban skies of Communist aeroplanes, and if those had been United States forces pinned down at the Girón estuary that would have happened, but because Girón was a CIA operation and the men on the ground were Cubans, aircraft of the United States armed services soared overhead, with loaded weapons, unwilling to assist.

In some areas the orthodox United States armed forces have been antagonistic towards the CIA. Old hands who have relied upon service-arm Intelligence services—and each service arm still maintains a vast Intelligence bureaucracy of its own—have viewed CIA personnel as dilettantes. They also tended to view clandestine operations as unnecessary, favouring in their stead the direct sledgehammer effect.

But even under the handicaps there have been some solid clandestine successes and despite additional restrictions by Congress, through the imposition of new checks, fresh guidelines to restrict CIA initiative further, there will probably continue to be other successes, and other failures.

Clandestine 'dirty tricks' while popularly associated with operations of the dimension of the Chilean, Indonesian, and Guatemalan affairs, actually more commonly and successfully involves no more than a small contingent of people. An agent, his superior, the director, whatever liaison personnel are required, and perhaps a national president, army general, politician whose fame has been founded upon anti-Americanism, but in any case a powerful national figure who accepts with open arms the money-filled attaché case.

'Dirty Tricks' have not necessarily or even preponderantly involved assassinations, support of armed insurgents, nor the systematical destruction of someone's reputation or credibility. The most consistent clandestine successes have been achieved without gunfire, and quite often without notice. Most often they have succeeded through bribery but there have also been any number of successful unobtrusive *coups*. For example in July of 1973 the KGB accomplished a tactical success for the USSR and hardly an eyebrow was raised.

Generally, the world scarcely took note that another small nation had fallen to the Soviets.

Afghanistan had been of strategic value to the Soviet Union ever since adjacent Iran became a Western bastion. In a professionally orchestrated *coup* which resulted in the swift overthrow of Afghanistan's King Mohammed Zahir Shah in July of 1973 the KGB was able to clear the way for the installation of its ardent sycophant, the Moscow-oriented leftist Sardar Mohammed Daud. Just that swiftly and competently did the KGB's clandestine undertaking make Afghanistan as much a Soviet satellite as any of the Balkan satrapies. It was one of those covert actions clandestine agents could applaud. The United States had only a short time before brought off a similar *coup* in Latin America, demonstrating that while the general understanding of 'dirty tricks' implied gunfire, murder, abduction, every unethical and underhanded attempt to achieve an end, in the main these had never been used.

Also, it was becoming increasingly difficult to differentiate between the variety of murder implied in the use of the term 'dirty tricks', and the kind of murder called proper. In Cambodia, for example, United States ground forces employed what was called a 'CBU-55' bomb (cluster-bomb-unit 55). This weapon not only fragmented, it also consumed all oxygen in a 100-foot radius. It was unlimited in its mayhem. Victims of the 'CBU-55' were considerably more varied than victims of poisoned tea or a silenced pistol. 'Dirty Tricks' in the classical interpretation of the term were never exclusive to the CIA. They were never exclusive to the worldwide Intelligence community, and the 'wet affair' resulting in murder—by whatever name it has been called, suicide, cardiac arrest, accidental death or assassination—has been an infinitesmal part of clandestine operations, regardless of popular opinion to the contrary. What has made it appear commonplace has been publicity. A nation could be skilfully subverted and providing there was no bloodshed, it rarely rated as a major news item; an old Bolshevik named Trotsky could be killed by an assassin using an alpenstock, and every newspaper on earth carried a feature story of the sinister implications.

A dozen high political officials in Egypt could be suborned, bribery and entrapment could neutralize or destroy two dozen French, German, British men of substance and influence and no one heard a word of it, but on a warm evening in the first week of September 1972, an Afghanistani named Monahajudin Gahiz, who published a newspaper in Kabul, was paid a visit by half a dozen men who arrived in a Soviet car. Two of those men entered the house and when the gunfire ended Monahajudin Gahiz and his nephew were dead. The assassins had been Russians. Their weapons were of Soviet manufacture and they allowed at least one witness to live. No attempt had been made to conceal anything. The clear warning was heeded. A year later Afghanistan became a Soviet 'protectorate', and while this caused hardly a ripple of interest the bloody murder of Monahajudin Gahiz was announced in newspapers throughout the world.

The mention of clandestine activity seems promptly to conjure up images of cloaks and daggers, and although one has become about as *passé* as the other the notion persists that covert operations to be worthwhile at all must have at least one silenced revolver and one cold-eyed espionage impresario.

20

Chiaroscuro

In the January 1969 edition of a United States quarterly review entitled *Foreign Affairs* an erudite contributor named William J. Barnds accurately noted that nothing the United States has done in recent years excluding its south-east Asian involvement created as much controversy as its headlong rush into the Intelligence field.

Barnds was well qualified to write this article. At one time he was connected with the CIA's Office of National Estimates, and later as a presumably dissociated staff member of the independent Council on Foreign Relations continued to attend Intelligence seminars and symposia.

Another Barnds statement could go unchallenged: the CIA is considered as either omnipotent and evil or as bumbling and incompetent. It has been accused of causing—secretly of course—every calamity of the last quarter century, and one of the surest ways to be left quite alone has been to defend the CIA.

The CIA has come to mean *the* United States Intelligence effort, while as a matter of fact, it is only *one* United States Intelligence agency. Others include the State Department's Bureau of Intelligence Research, the Pentagon's Defence Intelligence Agency and National Security Agency, as well as the Intelligence departments of the Army, the Navy, the Air Force, plus the Atomic Energy Commission's Intelligence units—and the FBI.

Condemnation of the agency has seldom arisen from specific knowledge, but that is one of those 'inalienable rights' free people enjoy. It has been repeatedly said over the past few years that most Intelligence functions are antiquated; that the 'spy' has been replaced by computer-telemetry and analysis. The facts are that aerial and electronic espionage, invaluable though they are, have definite limitations. Overflights produce photographs and taped radio transmissions, things which are subject to sophisticated camouflage and deliberate deception. The camera or computer which can reveal plans, plots or thoughts, has yet to be developed.

Aerial surveillance *is* important; it simply is not *all*-important. Hard Intelligence comes largely through spies, and ground-level espionage is as necessary to a nation as is its gross national product.

When international diplomacy seeks to succeed strictly from a basis in good will, it fails. When the good will is based on hard facts supplied by an agency such as the CIA, it succeeds. Good will did not convince the Soviets it would be to their advantage to remove the missiles from Cuba.

Naturally the CIA and other Intelligence agencies approve of people believing that computerized analysis—'clean espionage'—has largely replaced traditional methods for accumulating information. No one should expect them to react differently. But should the day arrive when the western world's remaining freedoms depend upon theoretical prognostications based upon educated guesses and newspaper clippings, the West will be two-thirds of the way towards extinction.

As far as approval is concerned, no one need actually approve of espionage any more than they are required to approve of multi-billion dollar warships and multi-million dollar warplanes, but they had better believe that in a largely hostile world survival depends more upon defence and good Intelligence than it does upon diplomacy and good will, and the CIA imperfect though it may be remains the West's best weapon in a cold war which has continued for thirty years after the hot war ended.

In early 1975 the Soviet Union conducted the most comprehensive war exercises ever conducted by a modern nation. They were in progress a full month and included every Soviet war-making capability, land-based, aerial and sea-going. Their purpose? A simulated nuclear attack upon the United States. No nation in history ever held such extensive (and hair-raising) exercises. They were monitored from beginning to end by the CIA—but news coverage was almost totally non-existent and for an excellent reason. The exercises were conducted under a massive news blackout. What would aerial surveillance have revealed? Only that the Soviet Union was engaging in general war exercises.

There is no reason to believe that the people of the Free World do not presently live in the most dangerous time in history. *Détente* for whatever it is worth aside, not a day passes in which we do not arise in the morning facing the possibility of nuclear attack before evening. America's foremost line of defence which in former times was the comforting expanse of two oceans is now the CIA and the nation's total Intelligence capability. Americans would benefit immensely if rather than running lemming-like behind false leaders and suspect prophets they began thinking in terms of strengthening and supporting the CIA through a system of adequate controls, something which no president from Harry Truman to Gerald Ford has been able to achieve.

This is where the trouble lies, and where it has existed for twenty years. The CIA has not only been able to penetrate the defences of our enemies but its expertise in this area has enabled it to penetrate and to an alarming degree dominate every control organization created to oversee it from the National Security Council to the Office of Management and Budget.

We need the CIA. What we do not need is another monolithic top-heavy staggeringly expensive bureaucracy running amok. Today more than ever before, because attack can come at any moment with devastating effect, the West must have a strong central Intelligence organization.

Every major city in the world possesses someone's referentura;* theirs, ours, or someone else's. Espionage has been recognizable for more than a decade as the most important instrument, more important than armies of soldiers or of diplomats. It has not been the negotiators who have kept armies marking time and missile bunkers closed, it has been what espionage has revealed about the

* 'Referentura' denotes the so-called 'dungeon' of every Soviet embassy in the world. It is a series of sound-proofed, windowless, very secret rooms which are the heart and brains of the embassies. All cipher and electronics espionage headquarters are in the referentura of each USSR embassy. Referentura personnel, a chief, a cryptographic clerk, and one deputy, man the quarters and these people are never allowed to leave a Soviet embassy unless heavily chaperoned. Nothing is allowed to be brought into a referentura and nothing is permitted to be taken out. Entrance is always through a steel door which is guarded round the clock by embassy military personnel. Referenturas are manned twenty-four hours a day. The term 'referentura' should not be confused with the Russian designation 'rezidentura' which means the KGB complement operating out of a Soviet embassy, but the 'rezidentura' in fact oversees many 'referentura' functions.

opposition's capability.

In 1952 the international trade in nuclear arms was $300 million by 1975 it had almost reached $18 *billion*. Everyone talks of peace, but in the Middle East where an Arab's most cherished possession in former times was the rifle he had bought at great sacrifice, there are now stockpiles of thousands of the latest Soviet automatic weapons available to anyone who expresses a desire to own one.

Everyone wants peace. The British have floating displays capable of travelling to any port-city in the world where prospective buyers can examine every possible kind of deadly weapon, all for sale.

Americans bearing palm branches have become the largest weapons merchants in the world. They have poignantly pleaded for peace in the chambers of the United Nations while simultaneously racking up sales of offensive weapons since about 1950 to the extent of $90 *billion*. In 1974 alone sales totalled slightly less than $9 billion.

The USSR sold almost $6 billion worth of offensive weapons in 1974, and prior to that time for the preceding twenty-four years averaged almost a billion and a half dollars in sales each year, mostly to nations with food, fertilizer, housing, medical and educational problems.

In the Middle East weaponry to replace what has been lost in the various flare-ups has brought Arab and Israeli treasuries to the brink of bankruptcy. In black Africa nationalists with no real enemies have spent close to $7 billion annually for weaponry most blacks cannot operate.

Another factor for trouble has been the seventy-four countries now in existence which did not exist prior to World War II. Each must have an army, an air force if it can raise pilots, and a navy if it has access to water. Also, each of these countries must make a choice, consciously or unconsciously as to which camp it will enter, East or West.

Arms are the tools of foreign policy. The USSR provides MiG-23 fighter-bombers to leftist régimes. The United States exports sophisticated aircraft and missiles to countries with anti-Communist governments. The Soviets challenge United States influence in the Middle East by courting Arab governments with dowries of weapons. They now have airfields available to them in Yemen, Afghanistan and Somalia, as a result of this kind of courting. The United States has supplied Spain, Iran, and until recently, Thailand, with weaponry in exchange for similar air-operational rights.

This East-West manoeuvring, challenging, posturing, is dangerous enough, but the increasing antagonisms along the Persian Gulf are a nightmare. Iran, having spent $8 billion for the best United States arms, now owns one of the most awesome arsenals in the world. Iran's leftist neighbour, Iraq, has been accumulating a Soviet arsenal as near to comparable as it can. They have been antagonists for centuries. So have Greece and Turkey, also enormously over-armed. So have the two Irelands, so have Israel and Egypt. And there is also a fresh peril, one which did not exist three years ago. Iran, the bristling Muslim nation could form an alliance with another Muslim state, Pakistan. Between them they could devastate India.

New alliances, fresh shifts of power, emerging ambitions, sputtering old antagonisms, and the disillusioning foot-dragging at the Strategic Arms Limitations Talks (SALT), support a valid doubt about the chances for peace. Since World War II there have been sixty armed conflicts resulting in the death of ten million people. All those wars were fought with modern weaponry, mostly imported.

It has been said there is no direct relationship between accumulated weaponry and war. Aside from the asininity of such a contention it could also be stated with a lot more possibility of truth that a world bristling with guns does not advance the prospects for peace, and meanwhile the people living along the perimeter can do nothing but provide themselves with the best possible defence, including the ability to know in advance from which direction attack may come, and more importantly provide themselves with the kind of extensive and efficient Intelligence organization which can, once it has verified the plausibility of attack by overflights, send in agents capable of dismantling someone's first-strike capability using any of the multiple choices available including coercion, blackmail, abduction or murder.

For the East there are at least a dozen KGB-affiliated Bloc Intelligence organizations. For the West there is the CIA and its supporting allied networks. Some day *détente* may progress to complete faith, trust and genuine good will. Until then, only those who wish the worst for the West will seriously advocate dismantling or neutering the Central Intelligence Agency, the West's best first line of defence.

Bibliography

Foreign Policies in a World of Change, by Joseph E. Black and Kenneth Thompson, publisher: Harper & Row, New York.

The Penkovskiy Papers, by Oleg Penkovskiy, translated by Peter Deriabin, publisher: Collins.

From Lenin To Malenkov, by Hugh Seton-Watson, publisher Praeger Company, New York.

The War Called Peace, by Harry and Bonaro Overstreet, publisher: W. W. Norton Co., New York.

KGB The Secret Work Of Soviet Secret Agents, by John Barron, publisher: E. P. Dutton Company, New York.

My Silent War, by Kim Philby, publisher: MacGibbon and Kee, London; Grove Press, New York.

Uncensored Russia, by Peter Reddaway, publisher: American Heritage Press, New York.

Soviet Defense-Associated Activities Outside The Ministry Of Defense, by James T. Reitz, publisher: Research Analysis Corp., Virginia.

The CIA And The Cult Of Intelligence, by Marchetti and Marks, publisher: Coronet, London, Alfred Knopf Co., New York.

Unmasked: The Story Of Soviet Espionage, by Ronald Seth, publisher: Hawthorn Books, New York.

The Politics Of Heroin In Southeast Asia, by Alfred McCoy, publisher: Harper & Row, New York and London.

Inside The Company—CIA Diary, by Philip Agee, publisher Penguin Books, London.

The Craft Of Intelligence, by Allen Dulles, publisher: Weidenfel and Nicolson, London; Harper & Row, New York.

Dagger In The Heart, by Dr Mario Lazo, publisher: Twin Cir Publishing Co. New York.

Additional sources consulted included magazine articles, newspaper reports and newscasts plus the means for substantiating them wherever possible, as well as other sources, all interesting but not all reliable. Understandably the subject does not lend itself to unemotional discussion nor to confessions or confidences. CIA policy prohibits co-operation on valid grounds, and although the agency is as fair as it can be actual detailed information of agency activities must come from other sources. Some of these are publicly available, others are not, but all have been exploited insofar as this has been possible.

Index